Marriage, Family Healing, and Wholeness

A Hmong Multicultural Pastoral Counseling Perspective

T. Cher Moua

© Copyright 2024 – All rights reserved.

It is not legal to reproduce, duplicate, or transmit any part of this document in either electronic or printed format. Recording or reproducing this document without prior authorization from the author is strictly prohibited.

Dedication

This work is dedicated to couples who want a dynamic relationship with each other and the Lord their God, seeking to be better communicators with each other and lovers of one another. They are relentless in their pursuit of each other, even through the darkest nights of their marriage journeys; they do not give up. They believe that with their faith in the Lord their God and the willingness of listening ears to lean in, to lend a listening ear to hear their struggles, to learn from each other, and to be patient to lead one another forward, they will succeed and flourish. They will thrive in their marriage journeys to glorify the Lord God and honor one another.

Also, this work is dedicated to Mai Yia, my lover, caretaker, companion, confidant, and defender. I have learned tremendously from her unrelenting, unwavering commitment to our marriage, even when things didn't go the way she wanted. She did not give up. She continues to put up with me and makes things work for the better. I learn so much from her. Additionally, I dedicate this work to all of my children and grandchildren for putting up with me as I learn to be the best father and grandfather in the best way I know how.

Finally, I praise the Lord my God through my Savior Jesus Christ and by the indwelling presence of the Holy Spirit, who continues to teach me about true and meaningful life. I have learned so much about what it means to be a good steward of what he has granted me.

Sola Gloria Deo!

Contents

Dedication	i
Steps Toward Marriage and Family Healing and Wholeness	1
Introduction	3
The Origin and Definition of Marriage	9
The Foundation of Marriage	20
The A's of Marriage Relationship	29
Biblical Covenant Definition	42
Marriage and Family Principles	62
Preference and Principles in Marital Relationships	72
Practicing Our Principles Instead of Functioning Out of Our Personal Preferences	76
Emotional Intelligence	92
Unconscious Bias	97
Self-talk - Self-Reflection/Evaluation	101
Facilitating Cross-cultural and Cross-Ethnic Marriages to Flourishing	106
Afterwords	124
Notes for Personal Reflections	127
About the Author	128

Steps Toward Marriage and Family Healing and Wholeness

The purpose of this work: To borrow Nathanael's question of Jesus when Philip told him about finding Jesus to be the Messiah from Nazareth: "*Can anything good come from there?*" - John 1:46. Maybe when you see my name attached to this work, you may have a similar skeptical question. "*Does this guy, T. Cher Moua, have anything good to say about Marriage and Family Healing and Wholeness?*" A good question, indeed. For anything to be trusted, especially ideas and propositions by people, the character and competency of the one who expounds have to be in congruence and coherent with what they say and must be based on personal experience and research. I was reminded by a friend that people nowadays do not take anything at face value anymore. They want "*scientific facts*" to back what is proposed, except when it comes from their point of view.

When I was younger and freshly entered the ministry, an old but wise pastor often reminded me, "*Young man. Preach only what you practice. And practice what you preach.*"[1] At the time, I felt somewhat annoyed by such a "*shallowed*" statement by such an old and "*less educated*" pastor. What does he know that I don't know? So went the rationale. I stopped analyzing my young and naive attitude. It was such an arrogant defense mechanism by an inexperienced and unwise young pastor who knew nothing about life and ministry (typical attitudes of the young and naive who think they know but do not know that they do not know). But as I grew older and began to reflect on this statement more intentionally and what the old pastor meant, it started to make

---

[1] As I get older and serve in ministry longer, I realize that the older generation, especially people who were "less educated" may not be as educated, but by life experience, they were so much wiser than the contemporary generation. The sentiment I have is that truth takes time to take roots and germinate. Overtime, the truth will spring up to life and transformation will begin. "Just give it time," as the saying goes.

sense (and took root in my life and practice) that verbal eloquence means nothing until and unless it's been lived out and proven. The following work combines my forty-plus years of marriage and thirty-plus years of marriage, family counseling, and mediation. I hope that this book will provide you with an insight or two to help you understand the relationship dynamics (as opposed to static) between spouses as you engage with their relationship.

This work aims to share biblical principles of marriage and family with you, the reader, hoping to present ideas on how to guide people who approach you for guidance in their marriage journeys. The principles expounded here are not infallible (only Scripture is infallible). This work intends to guide the reader and practitioner of Pastoral Counseling with knowledge that may help them flourish as they navigate their life's journeys.

Introduction

Each year, people celebrate Valentine's Day with flowers, candies, and cards. According to the National Retail Federation (NRF), consumers have spent a record amount of money on gifts ranging from flowers to cards to candies at a whopping $25.8 billion, an average of $186 per person, on Valentine's Day 2024[2]. This celebration has caught on to the Hmong and other communities worldwide. Each year, on February 14, people, especially Millennials, Gen X, and Z, look forward to this occasion with anticipation and excitement. People's expectations are high. Elaborated celebrations are planned. Everything from pastors preaching on "*love and relationship*" to secular folks gathering to indulge in binge eating and drinking. Alcohol is the desired and common beverage of choice for the occasion.

Those who have meaningful relationships anticipate with excitement the flowers and other gifts they will receive. But for those without meaningful relationships, the gloom and doom of the day is real. People have been committing suicide just because they do not have any meaningful relationship, or those who have are disappointed that their friends or spouses failed to buy them any flowers or gifts on this 'special' day - Valentine's Day. People are so rushed into doing things they have no clue about their reasons for doing what they do. Valentine's Day celebration, for example, the vast majority of people who celebrate have no clue as to the origin of this special day in the first place. This is the sad reality of our postmodern society.

So, what do we make of such a romantic, fantasy world? How can we bring people down from such a cloud of romance into the reality of life? This book is not intended to serve as a magic wand

---

[2] www.awarenessdays.com/valentines-day-2024. As the holiday continues to gain popularity worldwide, the demands would only increase, and people would spend increasingly more each year.

that can wave spells in your troubled relationship to make it disappear. Rather, it provides biblical principles for you to digest and practice so that you can grow in your quest for better relationships.

In the following pages, drawing from my personal experiences in marriage and premarital counseling, I aim to clarify the biblical foundations and principles of marriage. I hope to provide guidance on relationships within marriages and families. As you read and discuss the accompanying study questions, you will be inspired and challenged to invest more time and energy in your personal growth and your marriage, thereby minimizing heartache and disappointment in life.

"Steps toward marriage and family healing and wholeness?" Really? Who says that life is as simple and trivial as numeric numbers? Nowadays, the Do It Yourself (DIY) manuals, from how to change light bulbs around the house to changing the oil of your vehicles to a healthy lifestyle to a healthy marriage and family, are so easily accessible by just "*Ask Google.*" "*Do It Yourself*" is at our fingertips. All of us have used some or all of these guides. So, we are made to believe and practice because we do not want to make any mistakes in our "*fixing*" or "*installing*" anything in and around the house. Self-reliance and self-sufficiency are how to live in our postmodern, post-everything world. Life in this day and age has been reduced to technicalities. It's only about developing the technical skills needed to accomplish what you want. No more and no less. Anyone who thinks and acts otherwise is labeled as narrow-minded and unreasonable. Some are even being labeled as ignorant, arrogant, and intolerant bigots.

As societies have evolved, life and marriage have also evolved and can be categorized, redefined, and enumerated. If we just follow the directions, things would and should go according to plan. If things do not work according to plan, we do not understand or follow the directions. We are made to believe that whatever we do does not work because we have failed to understand the instructions or do not read them well.

In reality, life is much more than numerical numbers and technical skills. Life is complex. Marriage is difficult. Family dynamics are much more challenging than simply acquiring technical skills. How can we navigate the complexities of marriage and life? In the following pages, we are going to explore how life works, not from a human perspective, but from God's.

Before we dive into God's Word, though, let's get into the marriage relationship experience. Young and naive lovers do not think about the implications of marriage. Two strangers lay eyes on each other when they meet for the first time and just want to be together, without thinking about the compound and lasting ramifications and implications of their decision to be together. Courtship happens only at the physical level for the most part. As two strangers lay eyes on each other, their physical attractiveness catches on, and right away, they are convinced that their attractions were made in heaven. People are not aware of how they are wired and how this impacts their relationships and alters their future. They only think about the here and now. They do not have the tendency to think beyond the present.

Once they get married, they find out that marriage and married life require more effort than they anticipated. Marriage involves gives and takes. You give some and get some. Usually, the giving is more than the taking. It involves endurance to engage. Equip to empower. From a human perspective, this is counterintuitive. Our unspoken expectation is that when we get married, our spouse should give and give into our expectations and demands. This principle applies only to them, not us. We are selfish and do not really want to give, and we only want to receive. And, of course, we expect to receive. If we do not get what our unconscious mind wants, we become extremely angry and let our spouse "*have it.*"

We unconsciously assume that our spouses owe us everything because they "were given" to us to serve us and meet our "*needs*" instead of partnering with us on our journey in this life called marriage.

As we get older and become more mature in our relationships, I, for one, have come to realize that a dynamic marriage relationship requires a clear understanding of the meaning of marriage and its purpose, which is, as the marriage vows go:

> *"to have and to hold. For better or for worse. For rich and for poor. In health and sickness until death do us part."*

With this clearer understanding and acceptance of what the vows mean, relationships last longer, and married couples experience more tranquility.

Without a clear understanding of what marriage is, our engagement in marriage and the practice of marriage is bound to have conflicts because we do not realize the primacy of marriage principles. We bypass the principles entirely into practice, only conscious of our personal preferences. Usually, our marriage practice stems from our personal preferences instead of our principles. More on this later.

Being married have you ever thought about the meaning of marriage? What is marriage? What does it mean to be married? And who sets the rules of marriage? Are there any rules for marriage life to thrive and flourish? Marriage and married life is an assumption that those who engage in this ritual understand the fundamentals of marriage. But no one has seriously asked such questions and has a satisfactory answer.

As we continue to progress, we become accustomed to *"the new way"* of life, and we forget the fundamentals of human flourishing. We have forgotten the basic moral principles of love, respect, and honor - gender roles and responsibilities. We confuse ourselves with who we are as human beings and our different yet equally important roles for marriages to thrive and flourish. We engage in unnecessary debates about who should be the dominant one and who should be the submissive one. Who should lead boldly, and who should follow quietly and obediently? We engage in endless cycles of argument. No one wins. Everyone loses because none of us want to submit. Submission requires that we know our different roles and responsibilities and take them seriously, not as enslaving the other but as stewards of what God has delegated.

Further Conversations

1.   Discuss your understanding of courtship between a man and a woman in traditional and contemporary cultures. What are the differences between then and now? Please explain.

2.   Examine the significant influence of the current social, educational, economic, political, and technological *"advancement"* on courtship, engagement, and marriage dynamics on individual couples in different cultures and societies.

3.   Discuss the challenges and adjustments that couples may face during the early stages of marriage. How can knowing each individual's makeup and *"wiring"* help facilitate effective communication and conflict resolution skills to help navigate these transitions and minimize unwanted conflicts?

4.   Examine the impact of societal expectations and gender roles on marriage dynamics. How do traditional gender norms influence task division, decision-making processes, and power dynamics within marriage?

5.   Share with the group your own personal experiences through the journey of courtship, engagement, and marriage with those whose journey has just begun. What advice would you give to those who are planning for and/or looking at their marriage journey?

The Origin and Definition of Marriage

Nate Bagley, a blogger from the Gottman Institute, asks a rhetorical question, *"Seriously. What's the Point of Marriage?"* His answer? It is for growth. He quotes author Dr. David Schnarch, *Passionate Marriage,* who says that the goal of marriage is for growth and terms it 'The Human Growth Machine.' He goes on to quote another author, Finkel, who says that in our world, 'a new kind of marriage has emerged, one that can promote self-discovery, self-esteem, and personal growth like never before.' He agrees and says, *"I love the idea of having a growth-centered marriage. That is something I can achieve, and it feels satisfying to grow and improve. It is a tangible goal."*[3] Looking at this from an introspective (the *"Me"* first) perspective, it sounds great because it's an achievable goal for me to reach. It's tangible, but it's only about looking after ourselves and not about the interests of others. This proposition excludes the love component altogether. It forgets that humans are social creatures because we are created to be in relationships. We need growing, but more importantly, we must love and be loved.

Mr. Bagley expounds that how we treat our spouse has an impact on our personal growth, just like exercise. The more often we hit the gym, the stronger we would become. The more I give, the better I become. The unconscious ulterior motive is *"I do this to get that,"* which asks, *"What's In It For Me (WIIFM)?"* From a human perspective, that sounds pretty good. But how long can we continue to contribute to our personal growth without receiving feedback from our spouse and still keep on growing? Eventually, we would become exhausted in effort and energy and admit defeat because we could not give what we did not have. Period.

---

[3] www.gottman.com Nate Bagley, The Gottman Institute: "Seriously. What's the Point of Marriage?" A Research-based Approach to Relationship.

From a counseling perspective, as Robert F. Stahmann and William J. Hiebert's book, *Premarital & Remarital Counseling*, the primary motivations for marriage and remarriage are social expectations and personal gratification.[4] People get married because society expects them to *"start your family"* and their personal fantasy of *"If I get married, I will be happy or fulfilled."* How often does social pressure force people to "find that *person*" to get married because their age is "catching up" with them instead of thinking through the challenges marriage and family relationships will bring, and how can they be prepared to handle them? The consequence is often broken marriages mid-way through, with unintended consequences of family fragmentation and children as the victims of these pressures.

For us to know how to live productively without unnecessary problems, we need to take a step back and understand the foundational principles of marriage and embrace them as God has instituted. To understand marriage, we need to ask questions about the subject. What is marriage, what are the foundational principles of marriage (not just the personal preferences of Love Languages)[5] as expounded by other well-meaning and experienced marriage counselors, and why am I committing myself to this?

Christopher Ash pens the following statement about marriage as he understands it from a biblical perspective. He says, *"Marriage is the voluntary sexual and public social union of one man and one woman from different families. This union is patterned upon the union of God with his people, who are his bride, and Christ*

---

[4]Stahmann, Robert F. & Hiebert, William J. Premarital & Remarital Counseling. San Fransisco. 1997. Pages. 21-29.

[5]Chapman, Gary. The 5 Love Languages: The Secret to Love that Lasts. Chicago, IL. Moody Publishers, 1992, 1995, 2004, 2010.

with his church. Intrinsic to this union is God's calling to lifelong exclusive sexual faithfulness."[6]

Claire Smith, also from the TGC International Ministries, pens the following statement: *"To be made in the image of God is to be made as sexed and gendered humans, both male and female. This "sexual dimorphism" reflects the diversity and unity within the Trinity and shows us that we are made for each other. As male and female, humans have different roles and responsibilities that are grounded in the creation; he has responsibilities to lead, and she has responsibilities to accept his leadership and partner with him in fulfilling their joint mandate, relations that are most clearly worked out in the relationship of marriage. While sin entered the world by distorting gender differences, Jesus Christ came as a gendered human and opened the way for our genders and relationships to be redeemed. This does not allow for sex and gender to be redefined; rather, we are to live all the more faithfully within our roles and responsibilities indicated by our sex while sharing equally in the inheritance of Christ from God."*[7]

Right from the get-go, Scripture tells us that *"For this reason, a man leaves his father and mother and be united to his wife. And the two will become one flesh"* (Gen. 2:25). The question right away is, *"For what reason?"* The preceding verses give us the reason:

"The man said,

> *'This is now bone of my bones*
> *and flesh of my flesh;*
> *she shall be called 'woman,'*
> *for she was taken out of man.'* (Genesis 2:23-24)

---

[6] www.tgc.org A Biblical View of Marriage, Christopher Ash. TGC (The Gospel Coalition) International Ministries.
[7] Humanity as Male and Female. Claire Smith. TGC (The Gospel Coalition) International Ministries @ www.tgc.org

It's the man's acknowledgment of the woman as being a part of him. 'This is now bone of my bones and flesh of my flesh.' Notice the intricate relatedness between a man and a woman and yet the difference. '...bone of my bones and flesh of my flesh...' and 'she shall be called woman, for she was taken out of man.' This statement tells us that, yes, she was taken out of man. She was a part of man. Yet she is her distinctive person. So she is a part of man, but she is not a part of man. You get the picture.

First, marriage is a covenantal union between one man and one woman that is instituted by the Lord God. This is the basic principle of marriage throughout the history of civilization (with the understanding that most cultures of the world traditionally and biblically accept this view)[8]. God created two sexes - male and female - and united them into one. There is no such thing as a two-male or two-female marriage. The basic theological understanding of marriage is that it is reserved for men and women. This is the basic law of thriving human relationships. One surprising statement scripture makes in the New Testament is that *"The sting of death is sin, and the power of sin is the law"* (I Corinthians 15:56). The implication of this statement? Because of sin, all aspects of our relationships are *"dead."* Our relationship with God is dead. Our relationship with ourselves is dead. Our relationship with others is dead. All because of the sin committed by Adam and Eve.

The context here in 1 Corinthians 15 is about the resurrection of Jesus Christ as a precursor to the resurrection of the body. The need for the resurrection of the body is because of death. And

---

[8]My view of marriage relationship is both traditional and biblical. It should be noted that the advancement of philosophy, science, and technology lead contemporary societies to argue from a philosophical and technological points of view more so than the traditional, cultural, and biblical views. It is my conviction that marriage, based solely on the philosophical perspective would not bring flourishing into the marriage relationship because marriage and family flourishing are the foundation of society.

death came because of sin. And sin has a sting. And *"the sting of death is sin, and the power of sin is the law."* Notice the word *"law"* here. The Apostle Paul seems to suggest that death is a direct result of the poison of sin. But what the Lord God had commanded Adam and Eve was the law. What the Lord God uttered was the law. Anyone who violates the law of God will bear the consequences.

Scripture commented, *"For this reason, a man shall leave his father and mother and be united with his wife, and the two shall become one flesh"* (Genesis 2:23-24). We must affirm and accept that God's Word is that what he has spoken is firmly established. To put it into contemporary language: *"the buck stops"* with God. Another scripture affirms that God's Word is flawless (Proverbs. 30:5). When Jesus came on the scene, he reaffirmed the endurance of God's Word (Matthew 24:35; Mark 13:31; Luke 21:33). Based on this foundational truth, we must accept and live by God's principles unwaveringly.

The main reason for sex between a man and a woman is for procreation. God commanded Adam and Eve to *"increase and multiply"* (Genesis 2:16-18) and therefore glorify God. Without the sex differences, as some have rightly pointed out, there would not be the possibility of procreation. God created them male and female for this specific purpose - to multiply and increase in number and fill the earth. To be multiplied and fill the earth requires both sexes.

The understanding that marriage is God-instituted leads us to think more deeply about and value this institution highly. The deeper our understanding is, the more we value, appreciate, and learn to be better stewards of what God has instituted and given. It comes down to stewardship of how we live out our marriage vows. So, the understanding or perspective we choose to take will lead us to live accordingly because everything we do in life has consequences.

Society trains us to think and behave, which is how we will consciously and unconsciously live out our belief system. On the other hand, if we allow ourselves to be trained by Scripture, we will believe what Scripture says and live by Scriptural principles. Instead of allowing society to shape our thinking and perspective about marriage and life, we will let Scripture shape our worldview, sharpen our focus on life, and live out God's Word daily, both personally and in marriage.

In our postmodern, post-Christian, post-moral, post-everything, marriage has been and continues to be defined as a union between two (or more) consenting people whom the government legalizes for social and economic benefits. Marriage is defined only socially and economically. Socially, any two (or more) people who are *"in love"* with each other can and should marry if they feel like it, and the government should grant their request/desire.

Economically, people who cohabit feel the need to *"get married"* because their economic interests hang in the balance. They need to think about the hard work they put into *"building"* their *"home"* and their accumulated assets together. As such, they need to have a legal bind so that no one except the "married couple" themselves has the right to what they have accumulated. They don't think about marriage beyond that and the ramifications of their decisions because they do not have the basic moral foundations of life as human beings. That's why people push for the legalization of marriage across the board.

Due to the government's involvement in morality and ethics, society shifts its foundational principle of life to relative rules and regulations. It shifts our understanding of morality to become social justice and equality. We are taught to believe that human governments can regulate and sanction morality and ethics when, in fact, basic morality is intrinsic. Morality is intrinsic in the sense that even non-religious people believe that there is such a thing as *"The Golden Rule"* of *"do to others as you would have them done to you." And "Do not murder. Do not steal."* We are influenced to believe there is no absolute to anything because society is God-void, human-focused, and centered. Everything can be regulated and sanctioned according to our liking.

We have slowly but surely forgotten about the *"eternity"* the Lord God has written in each of the human hearts (Ecclesiastes 3:11). Whether a person subscribes to the biblical values or not, this Scripture testifies that God has written eternity in the hearts of all human beings. Whether they are atheists, non-religionists, or pantheists, this basic morality is written in their hearts.

We forget that our hearts' yearning is the fulfillment of the Lord God's original design and desire for human flourishing. The human flourishing designed by the Lord God is not only social-exclusive but spiritual as well. By regulating and sanctioning marriage, we are making ourselves gods. We replace the Lord God with ourselves. We are *"Playing God"*[9] in every aspect of life. We are not only slapping God in the face but stumping the Lord God under our feet and telling him that his original design does not fit our liking. We are smarter and wiser than he is. This is a total affront to the Lord God Almighty.

From a human perspective, we cannot. Life is much more than technical parts; it is to be taken piece by piece and step by step and replaced by any broken or unfit piece. In short, we cannot pick and choose. We have to embrace and take the whole or not at all.

At first glance, these steps seem too simple to be realistic. For the most part, people who started marriage and family just jumped with their two feet into it, hoping there would be a place for them to land. However, some people find their marriage relationships to be a bottomless pit; they cannot find any place to rest their feet, let alone stand on solid ground. For most people, marriage is a result

---

[9]Crouch, Andy. Playing God. Inter Varsity Press. Downers Grove, IL. 2013, Crouch describes the use and misuse of power. Crouch explains in detail about the power of power and the use of power and its ramifications.

of falling in love with strangers who become their partners. What they do not realize is that life is much more than walking on clouds when they *"fall"* in love with each other. Marriage and life are much more than just getting to *"know"* each other and sharing one another's hopes and dreams, hoping everything falls into place. There is no such thing as *"Living Happily Ever After."* Marriage involves much more than pure romance or recreational sex to satisfy one's emotional needs. It involves hard work, which we will discuss later.

As a confessed Christ-follower, I am reminded of Jesus' Words in Luke 6:47-49 NIV digital version,

> *"As for everyone who comes to me and hears my Words and puts them into practice, I will show you what they are like. They are like a man building a house who dug down deep and laid the foundation on rock. When a flood came, the torrent struck that house, but could not shake it because it was well-built. But the one who hears my Words and does not put them into practice is like a man who built a house on the ground without a foundation. The moment the torrent struck that house, it collapsed, and its destruction was complete (emphasis added)."*

The context here is about faith in Jesus Christ. Jesus said,

> *"...everyone who comes to me and hears my Words and puts them into practice... They are like a man building a house, who dug down deep and laid the foundation on the rock."*

Notice at least three principles: First, those who come to him. Coming to Jesus is a personal conscious decision. Believing in Jesus is not a blind faith. It is a conscious decision because Jesus is not just some kind of force but a Person. Jesus is God becoming Man. He lived and died. Buried, and rose, again from the dead, ascended to heaven and promised to return to earth when his time was right.

> *"What is more, God's Word promises that everyone who received him and believed in his name, he gave them the right to become children of God"* – (John 1:12).

Because of these truths, those who believe in him will be held accountable in terms of awards and accountabilities. These are the basic tenets of the Gospel. Yes. We believe that Jesus is God coming in the flesh to die for the sins of the world, and anyone who believes in him shall not perish but have eternal life. That's true. But how many put his Word into practice? When he says, Love others as you love yourself. Or treat others as you would like to be treated. Do we obey or not?

Second, those who hear his Words. Jesus said that unless the Father drew anyone, they would not come to him. However, no one would come to Jesus without hearing his Word. *"For faith comes from hearing the message, and the message is heard through the word about Christ"* – (Romans 10:17). Only those who hear his call and realize their needs would surrender themselves and come to him. Coming to Jesus is both a call and a choice. The call is initiated by Christ through the Holy Spirit.

The choice, on the other hand, is about the person who hears the voice of God tugging their hearts. It is up to us to make the move in response to God's call and take a step. We have been given free will. We can choose to accept God's invitation or reject it. Many people who come to Jesus do not necessarily hear his clear calling. They may hear his voice but do not understand the clear content of his call. Hearing Jesus' Words means that we must pay attention to the meaning of what he says.

Third, those who put his Words into practice. It's not enough to just come to Jesus. Meaning a person who hears the Gospel proclaimed and understood God's love through the death, burial, and resurrection of Jesus for their sins. Confessed their sins and accepted Jesus as their Savior and Lord as Scripture repeatedly declares,

"Those who accept him and those who believe in his name, he gave them the right to become children of God." (John 1:12).

And, *"The one is in Christ is a new creation. Behold, the old has gone, and the new has come." II Corinthians 5:17.* Coming to Jesus is the first step. When we come to Jesus, we must hear his Words.

Hearing his Words requires that we listen. Paying attention to the content of his words. Listening to his Words regularly is the foundation for our growth. Then, learning to put his words into practice. It's not enough just to come to him and hear his Words; it is critically important to put his Words into practice. Learning to learn how to practice God's Word daily. That's why Jesus said to Satan,

"Man shall not live by bread alone but by every word that proceeds from the mouth of God" (Matthew. 4:10).

God's Word is food for the soul. Just like we need daily food to nourish and sustain our physical life, so we need spiritual food to sustain our spiritual life if we are to not only survive but succeed. Obedience to God's Word is most important. God's Word is also a sword in our battle against the enemy because Scripture calls the believer and follower of Jesus Christ, a soldier. As soldiers in the army, we need the full armor of God (Ephesians. 6:10-17). But it's not enough to have all of the gears but lack the skills to use them. It does not matter how complete or powerful the armor is. Unless you know how to use them, they are useless.

Yes. God's Word is food for the soul and sword for the battle. It does not matter how much food we have on the table; if we do not take it and eat it, it is useless. Unless we digest what's on the table, our bodies will not benefit. And we can have plenty of swords, but they are useless unless we know how to use them. Ultimately, we will fall victim to the lack of skills needed to use them. Period.

God's Word is also *"a lamp to our feet and a light to our path"* (Psalm 119:105). No one in their right mind would walk in the dark of night without any lamp or light. They would not intentionally stumble and fall to hurt themselves. They would not throw themselves off the cliff of despair. However, people do stumble and fall, and circumstances that cause them to stumble may be out of and beyond their control. But there are those who just refuse to accept the lamp of God's Word to light on their paths. God's Word reminds us that God's Word is readily available for those who accept and use it to light the way on their journey.

Anyone who does not want to stumble on their journey must have a lamp to shine on their feet and a light to brighten their path when the nights fall and darkness takes over. This marriage journey is hard. The nights are dark, and the days are long. Without enduring a lamp, you will stumble when night falls, and the batteries of your lamp run out on your journey. What would you do without the eternal lamp of God's Word?

The Foundation of Marriage

People who claim to believe in Jesus but live like non-Christians are not being truthful. They also make God out to be a liar because their actions contradict their professed faith, as stated in 1 John 1:10. What does it look like to live by God's Word? It means that God's Word must be the foundational principle guiding our lives and actions. God's Word must be the nourishing element of our life. Unless our heart is impacted and transformed by the Word of God, there is little else we can do. God's Word is clear and tells us that the human *"heart is wicked and deceitful above all things and beyond cure"* (Jeremiah 17:9). No one can understand the heart condition, except the Creator of the heart – the Lord God himself. Fast forward to the New Testament and focusing on Jesus's words, he said, *"... the mouth speaks what the heart is full of"* (Matt. 12:34). Unless the heart is reformed and transformed, the work of the hands would be futile. That is why our efforts in building a house are futile unless the Lord Himself is in the center and serves as the Architect.

Scripture is clear:

> *"Unless the Lord builds the house,*
> *the builders labor in vain.*
> *Unless the Lord watches over the city,*
> *the guards stand watch in vain.*
> *In vain you rise early and stay up late,*
> *toiling for food to eat—*
> *for he grants sleep to those he loves."*
> *(Psalm 127:1-2) (Emphasis added).*

First of all, what is a house? Why do we need to build a house? A house is a shelter for safety and security. It is a place where people or animals congregate to rest and rejuvenate. A house is where family members come together to connect and nurture their social, emotional, mental, and spiritual relationships. We need to build a house as a place to call home. A place to put our roots down. A place where we can come to. Without a house, we would be wandering without any secure place to put down roots. Without any firm roots, there would not be any flourishing. The building of a house is foundational to human flourishing.

This Scripture talks about the foundation of marriage because it is the start of family, and family is anchored in the house. A house is built to become a home. A home then becomes the center for building and growing a family. It is where children will be born and nourished to flourish. It is where the community begins. Hence, "Home is where the heart is." The question is, why is the Lord's role in building a house so important? Disasters and destructions are a part of the human experience. To prolong life and provide safety and security, a strong shelter has to be erected/built. Because the Lord God is the Creator, He alone knows the strength of storms, what to do, and how to do it to withstand the storms of life.

This Psalm tells us that the Lord is the Builder. He is the Architect of marriage. Marriage is instituted by the Lord God. It says,

> *"Unless the Lord builds the house..." "Unless..."*

Scripture says. The Lord is the only sure Architect. As house-builders, we can do all we want, but nothing is going to be a sure foundation because of our limited knowledge of the ground below. We do not know where the strongest point of the ground is and how firm our building construction is.

This means that we need to give the Lord permission to build our houses. We have to admit our inadequacies. Our incompetence. Our inability to build a strong and lasting house. We lack the skills. We lack the materials. We lack the strength. We lack what is needed to build a strong and lasting house. We must allow the Lord to build our houses for us. We need to permit Him to build the house that is best suited for us. Have you ever admitted your inadequacies to the Lord? This, in Scripture, is called repentance. Repentance requires that we acknowledge our inability to do anything worthwhile and turn away from that attitude and behavior.

We are the subcontractors. In the commercial world, subcontractors must agree to the terms and conditions set by the general contractor. They follow the blueprints of the building plan thoroughly and according to the vision of their architect. Similarly, we have to seek advice from the Architect of our world. Then, build a sustainable house. At the same time, we need to surround ourselves with reliable subcontractors (people) who agree to and follow the blueprints of the Architect, that is God Almighty. And, of course, we must live up to His contract.

Because the Lord is the Builder of the house, we must not only consult Him regarding the building of this house called marriage and family. We must rely on His wisdom as to what kind of building materials to use to build our building so that, in the words of Jesus again,

"When a flood came, the torrent struck that house but could not shake it, because it was well-built." - Matthew 6:48 (emphasis added).

In marriage relationships, especially relationships that are rooted in Christ, everything we say and do must be measured by God's Word and how we live up to His standard of a loving relationship. As He said, *'If you love me, you will obey my commandment.'*

Unless Jesus is the foundation and center of our marriage, we will inevitably face difficulties. It's only a matter of time. How can we handle these challenges without wisdom from above?

Marriage is more than just "living happily ever after." It involves the highs and lows of life—the exhilarating moments on the mountaintops and the disappointments and challenges in the valleys. Can you share some of the mountaintop exacerbations and valleys of heartaches you have experienced in your marriage? How about your "valley of the shadow of death" experiences so far? Even if you long to share your aches and pains, is there anyone willing to listen? Or would there be anyone whom you trust enough to share without fear of your confidence being violated?

It involves hard work. Investing. Sacrificing. Giving and Receiving. Patience. Kindness. Goodness. Peacefulness. Forgiveness. Repentance. Reconciliation. Renewal.

But most importantly, Recognize. Recognize that marriage is not just our desire to be with the other person. It is instituted by the Lord God. His purpose for marriage is much more than we understand or care to understand.

Psalm 127 continues:

"In vain you rise early and stay up late, toiling for food to eat - for he grants sleep to those he loves."

What have you done so far that has not been in vain from an eternal point of view? What do we do, busy toiling all of our lives? Isn't it just for food? So, this Scripture reminds us of a life void of the presence of God. Without God's superintendence, all of our work, including marriage relationships, is in vain. Sleepless nights would be the lot of those who have no fear of the Lord God. We toil to eat. We toil to preserve our relationship, but in vain. The Lord God grants sleep to those whom he loves - and loves him. Without the Lord God, it would only be as the Hmong say, *"Ua caav lwj sis ib ruaqhov muaj tej mivnyuas - be like rotten stumps leaning on each other because of the children."* As one woman said to me several years ago when she and her husband went through their marriage difficulties, "Pastor, now I realize that I cannot live with him, but I cannot live without him either."

For the Christ-follower, marriage and the marriage covenant requires the fruit of the Spirit. Paul says,

> *"But the fruit of the Spirit is **love, joy, peace, forbearance (patience), kindness, goodness, faithfulness, gentleness and self-control** (Emphasis added). Against such things, there is no law" (Galatians 5:22-23).*

Notice that these are not "gifts" but "fruits." What's the difference between a fruit and a gift?

Love. Joy. Peace. Forbearance/Patience. Kindness. Goodness. Faithfulness. Gentleness. Self-control. What do these mean in practical terms? What does each of these contribute to the well-being of our marriage relationship? It would be good to reflect on these individually and appropriately put them into practice in our daily lives.

Love - What is love? Everybody regularly uses the word. But do we know the actual meaning of the word? Why is love so important? Scripture tells us that:

> *"Love is patient. Love is kind. It does not envy. It does not boast. It is not proud. It is not rude. It is not self-seeking. It is not easily angered. It keeps no record of wrongs. Love does delight in evil, but rejoices with the truth. It always protects. Always trusts. Always hopes. Always perseveres"* (I Corinthians. 13:4-7).

If love is defined as an attribute and attitude of God, how do we receive it? So love, when translated into the human level, is the fruit of the Spirit, according to Galatians 5:22-23. If love is a fruit of the Spirit of God, how do you receive it? How do you bear this fruit? It is logical that if love is a fruit of the Spirit, he would have to bear it in and through the life of the believer. Bearing this fruit is to bow to the Lord of love and be filled with His character. Scripture says that God is Love. God is the originator of love. It's easy to gloss over this foundational principle because we think that we know what it means. We often overlook the significance of love because we believe we've been practicing it all our lives and don't need reminders of its meaning. However, *"He who lives in love lives in God, and he who lives in God lives in love."* Scripture says that only those who live in God live in love. But how do we live in God? Are there any technical steps we can take to get close to and live in God?

Joy

Joy is the second fruit of the Spirit. How do you get joy? As we follow the logic of Scripture, love is one of the fruits of the Spirit. Similarly, joy is also a fruit of the Spirit. True joy has to be borne by the Spirit of God. Scripture tells us that joy comes from the Lord. Nehemiah reminds his people (and us) that,

"The joy of the Lord is (our) strength." (Nehemiah 8:10).

True joy comes only from and through our relationship with the Lord Jesus. This joy originates with and in Jesus and Jesus alone. We can say that we have "joy," but our "joy" without Christ is fleeting. All of us experience life's ups and downs regularly. Relative joy comes in the good times, but true joy comes even in the bad times of our lives. True joy is not dependent on our circumstances but despite them, because our joy comes from the Lord. The joy of the Lord is our strength.

Peace

Shalom - peace - can only come through Jesus Christ. The Bible describes Jesus as the Prince of Peace who would be born into Israel as Isaiah the Prophet proclaimed: "For to us a child is born. To us, a Son is given. And the government will be on his shoulders. And he will be called Wonderful Counselor, Mighty God. Everlasting Father. Prince of Peace" (Isaiah 9:6). This Scripture reminds us of at least one truth: Since sin entered the world and affected humanity, the whole creation has been and continues to be in conflict with itself. Before the birth of the Prince of peace, there was constant conflicts. Until, this "Child" was born and this "Son" was given.

How do you get peace? Jesus said,

"In the world, you will have trouble, but take heart. I have overcome the world." "Peace, I leave with you. My peace, I give to you." (John 14:27; 16:33).

The only way to true peace in and through conflicts is in Jesus Christ. This takes time and effort. Surrender and submission. His peace will not come to those who do not want it, are not willing to receive it, and fail to appropriate it. True peace, as Jesus puts it in the Gospel of John, is not the absence of conflict but, in and through conflicts, the peace that Jesus gives will endure.

Patience

How do you acquire patience? What is patience? Scripture tells us that patience is different in the mind of God and man. In the mind of man, it is seen as slowness, while in the mind of God, he is not willing that anyone should perish but that all would come to repentance (II Peter 3:9). Patience, according to God's Word, is an attribute of character. It is developed by attuning ourselves to the Spirit of God and saturating our hearts and minds with the Word of God. Not just reading but chewing on it constantly and consistently. Over time, God's Word will shake us, shape us, and sharpen us to become like Christ in our thoughts and actions.

Kindness

How do you live out kindness in your life? Being aware of the kindness you have received is the first step toward living a kind life.

"We love because he first loved us" (I John 4:19).

Similarly, we extend kindness because it was initially shown to us by Him. Showing kindness to others is essentially reflecting the kindness of the Lord God that we've experienced in our own lives.

Goodness

What is goodness? What is the difference between goodness and badness? What are some of the traits of a bad person? In comparison to the badness of a person, what is the goodness of a person? How do you know if a person is living out the goodness of God? The Oxford Dictionary defines *"Goodness"* as *"the quality of being morally good or virtual." "The quality of character or conduct that entitles the possessor of approval and esteem."* With this definition, then, how do we live our lives so that our goodness is observed and approved without us telling people?

Faithfulness

What is faithfulness? Can you measure faithfulness? Faithfulness is a character trait that endures. A faithful person remains faithful, unwavering in their commitment to a life-long journey. They would not waver or quit when the going gets tough. They continue to endure to the end, for they know that this life is a journey. They know as soon as they set foot on a path, sooner or later, they will surely reach their destination. With this hope in their hearts and minds, they continue until they reach their destination.

Gentleness

What is the difference between gentleness and harshness? Gentleness is a quality of character that exhibits tenderness and kindness. To be gentle is to be tender both in attitude, behavior, and action. It's not demanding or even perceived to be demanding.

People can feel your gentleness or harshness. The way we communicate, our tone of voice, and our manners can come across as gentle or harsh.

Self-control

What does it take exhibit *"self-control?"* Self-control is the harvest of the fruit, if you will. If you achieve self-control, you have achieved your goal or the goal that the Spirit of God has for you as a new plant in God's garden. You now have the harvest of the new plant (which is your new life in Christ). Self-control is a character trait that exhibits completeness, which means that self-control is a process. It starts with love and progresses through joy, peace, and love, until it culminates in self-control.

All of these qualities of character do not happen overnight. They require the cultivating of the soil, the planting of the seed, tending to the condition of the plant, and caring for the plant until it grows to maturity so it bears fruit. All of these qualities of character require that we allow our hearts to be cultivated so that the seed of God's Word can fall into the good soil of the heart. Then, as the seed of God's Word is planted, we allow it to germinate and take root. As the Word of God takes root in our hearts and grows, we need to continue to weed out. Weeds are inherently unwanted. Weeds to choke the tender shoots of God's Word so that they grow to maturity. These are critically important parts of God's Word that work in our lives to bear fruit that will last.

Then, marriage is also like a city. In the ancient world, a city was built with a wall around it. The city leaders would appoint guards on the city walls for security. Only powerful weapons and diligent guards can protect the city from being invaded by enemy forces. Scripture says,

> *"Unless the Lord watches over the city, its watchmen stand guard in vain."* This confirms Jesus' words to his disciples: *"Abide in me and I in you...for apart from me you can do nothing"*
>
> *(John 15:1-6).*

As we can see from Scripture, everything we do revolves around our foundation. The kind of foundation we have, or lack of it, to build our houses/homes will determine their durability and flourishing.

The A's of Marriage Relationship

A part of the marriage covenant is the following ten steps. If we can put these principles into practice, our marriages will thrive amid challenges and chaos.

1) Awareness

"I did that?" Notice that this is a question, not a statement. What's the difference between a question and a statement? Let's discuss this difference to become more conscious of our surroundings. A question seeks to understand the other person's reception of our actions and reactions, which enhances our effectiveness in engaging with ourselves and others. A statement, on the other hand, assumes awareness of our words and actions. However, depending on the tone, it can be perceived as either hostile or defensive.

Being aware of yourself and your surroundings requires you to stop talking and start listening—intentionally. Listen well before speaking; restraining yourself is the number one challenge. Are you aware that you are married? And that you are married to the person beside you right now? Are you consciously aware of their presence in your life? This is your position: that you are not alone anymore, that you are not single anymore. This self-awareness should begin to change your attitude. More on this self-awareness later.

Dr. John Townsend, in his book *People Fuel*, spends four chapters describing what I call the *"4L principles"* and categorizes them into quadrants. [10]

- Quadrant 1: Be Present
- Quadrant 2: Convey the Good
- Quadrant 3: Provide Reality
- Quadrant 4: Call to Action.

The 4L Principles

Understanding and practicing these principles can enhance relationships between spouses:

L1 - Leaning In

Being present and paying attention. As a married couple, how readily do we lean in while the other is talking? Often, we are not consciously willing to lean in, which means we do not fully hear or understand what the other person is saying. Leaning in requires intentional engagement, signaling to your partner that you are permitting them to engage. Engagement is a critical part of conversations, and leaning in is crucial for effective communication.

---

[10] Townsend, John. People Fuel: Fill Your Tank for Life, Love, and Leadership., Grand Rapids, MI. Zondervan, 2019. Pp. 82-153.

L2 - Listening To

Focus on both the content and the context. In relationships, not just marriages, people often fail to listen. Without leaning in, the likelihood of truly listening is minimal. We may hear noises or words but do not grasp the content. In everyday conversations, people beg us to hear them—not just their words but the meaning behind them. When we do not listen, we fail to understand the conversation's content and context.

L3 - Learning From

If we acknowledge our ignorance, we become willing to learn. Learning from others involves asking the right questions to gain the correct information and instruction rather than merely telling. Learning from means that we must consciously aware of our presumed biases, taking control of our impulsive urge to answer. It means we must refrain from being "prepared" to answer. Instead being attentive to the speaker's intentionality and how their message is communicated.

L4 - Leading Forward

To lead, you must know the way. It's not enough to just *"show the way."* Scripture says no one has gone into heaven except the one who came from heaven. Only the one who came from heaven can lead others back to heaven (John 3:13). Similarly, to lead effectively with credibility and integrity, you must be one step ahead to see what lies ahead and also understand the followers' surroundings. You cannot lead others to where they need to go if you have not already been there and do not know the way. You need to understand your subject and back up your words with actions.

Putting These Principles into Practice

How do you put these into practice? They sound good, but implementing them is a challenge. Here is a simple yet effective way to start: Be **INTENTIONAL**! Intention is key, and this comes back to awareness. More on this self-awareness later. If you are unaware of what you are doing or saying, you will not know how to pay attention. Attention takes patience, an important ingredient of love. Being patient means standing strong and immovable in the face of annoyance. Do not let others' *"unreasonable demands"* affect you.[11]

Further Conversations

1.   Define the 4L Principle of Leaning in, Listening to, Learning from, and Leading forward in the context of personal and marital relationships according to your understanding. How do these principles contribute to marriage and family flourishing?

2.   Explore the concept of Leaning in and its significance in building trust and rapport in marriage and family relationships. What does it mean to lean in, and how does it promote active engagement and connection with others, especially your spouse?

3.   Discuss the importance of Listening to your spouse in fostering empathy, understanding, honor, and respect. How do

---

[11] These principles were developed during and through my SLI training by Cru leadership development. I have learned valuable lessons regarding this 4L principle and it works in inter personal as well as cross-cultural contexts when properly employed but it takes focus. I am grateful for the investment Cru LDHR put into me and my cohort for the development of leadership to better serve the kingdom of God.

effective listening skills enhance communication and promote positive interactions in your marriage relationship?

4. Reflect on the principle of Learning with and from your spouse and yourself and its role in personal growth and development. How do spouses benefit from learning from each other's backgrounds, experiences, and perspectives?

5. Examine the concept of Leading forward and its implications for taking action and driving positive change in your marriage and family. How do couples demonstrate leadership and co-leadership qualities by inspiring each other, fostering collaboration, and contributing towards meaningful progress and flourishing?

6. Discuss the interplay between the 4L principles and other factors such as emotional intelligence, conflict resolution, and teamwork. How do these principles complement and reinforce each other in fostering healthy and productive relationships? Is there such a thing as *"teamwork"* in a marriage relationship? Why or why not?

7. Reflect on the challenges and barriers to embodying the 4L principles in personal and marital relationships. What factors might hinder couples from effectively leaning in, listening to, learning from, and leading forward, and how can they overcome these obstacles?

8. Explore the cultural and societal influences on the 4L principles. How do cultural norms (even from the same ethnic group), values, and communication styles shape individuals'

approaches to leaning in, listening to, learning from, and leading forward in relationships?

9. Discuss the implications of the 4L principles for marriage and family cultivation for development and flourishing. How can couples cultivate a culture that embraces these principles to foster collaboration and growth toward flourishing?

10. Reflect on your own experiences and beliefs regarding the 4L principles in relationships and marriage roles. How do these principles align with your personal values and experiences, and how do they shape your approach to building meaningful connections and driving positive change in your life and your family?

11. How can individuals and couples cultivate a mindset of continuous learning (which requires humility and openness), collaboration, and forward-thinking to achieve their goals and aspirations?

2) Acknowledgment

"Yes, I did that." Acknowledging our actions is critically important in a marriage. Often, pride prevents us from admitting our mistakes, hindering personal growth. Overcoming this requires humility and self-awareness. It means *"killing"* our ego and *"dying to sin with Christ."* As the Apostle Paul said, "

> *I have been crucified with Christ, and I no longer live, but Christ lives in me. The life I now live in the body, I live by faith in the Son of God, who loved me and gave himself for me"*
> (Galatians 2:20).

Being crucified with Christ means being aware that He lives in you, empowering you to live a life that honors Him. This should be your practice.

3) Admission

"I did that, and I was wrong." Admitting our mistakes requires authenticity and understanding the consequences of not doing so. Unacknowledged wrongs increase our pain and deepen the divide between us and our partners. An unapologetic attitude widens the chasm in our marriage and leads to emotional isolation.

Conversely, having the courage to admit your shortcomings can liberate you from sleepless nights and prolonged struggles in your marriage. Acknowledging your wrongs and accepting God's grace is freeing. It takes courage to admit faults and accept correction from others. Over the years, I've learned that your response to correction can have two outcomes: seeing it as criticism can make you bitter and stunt your growth while viewing it as constructive feedback can help you learn, grow, and improve your behavior and approach.

4) Acceptance

"I accept responsibility for my actions." Taking responsibility for your actions means not blaming others for your emotions. Pay attention to your emotions and understand their role in your well-being. Accept full responsibility for what happens in your life and acknowledge your partner's presence in it. Remember, you cannot change your partner's attitude or actions—only influence them, and this should be done consciously. Accept your partner as they are without expecting them to change to fit your preferences. Acceptance should be without rationalization or defensiveness; as conditional acceptance is hard to accept.

5) Adaptation

Adaptation requires effort from both parties. Growing up in different cultures and backgrounds means we've learned different ways of operating. These methods are not necessarily wrong; they are simply different. Consider what differences each of you bring to the relationship. Are you aware of them? Can you discuss them calmly?

"I am willing to change and accommodate you." Be open to letting others into your world, even if their entry makes you uncomfortable or fearful because it's unfamiliar. In marriage, people will see the dark and ugly rooms of your life—that's part of the commitment. Be willing to accommodate your spouse, be vulnerable, and hide nothing. This builds trust, especially after it has been broken. Interestingly, we often accommodate outsiders to be accepted, yet resist accommodating our spouses. We feel entitled to our place and position, expecting others to accommodate us without reciprocating.

6) Adjustment

"What can I do to serve you better?" Be willing to adjust. When your spouse asks you to change, be open to discussing which areas you can improve. Recognize what you need to let go of and what you need to change. Adjust your language, tone, and communication style. Adjustment is a part of life that we must embrace intentionally to grow. If change seems difficult or unfair, ask for help: "Can you help me change?"

7) Assimilation/Acculturation

Assimilation means letting go of what you once held onto and embracing the unfamiliar. A marriage relationship is all about assimilation and acculturation. We let go of our single life and monocultural ways, embracing life as a couple. We bridge our cultural backgrounds, embracing each other's customs and manners. We embark on a new journey, learning thoroughly and comprehensively about each other, including our respective families and cultures.

As we marry and potentially have children, we blend these elements to create a new family culture. We assimilate into each other's lives, forming a new entity known as a family, and consciously decide to move forward together.

Facing the future together, without knowing what lies ahead, requires a commitment to work on our desire to assimilate. Whatever challenges arise, face them together with sincerity. Share your heart's desires, pains, and hurts. Work towards solutions that benefit both of you. Go beyond each other's expectations in showing love and dare to do things that have never been done before.

8) Assessment

"How are we doing? What have we done? What are we doing? How can we improve our relationship moving forward?" Regularly check in on your relationship. Can you discuss disappointments and frustrations calmly? After a few days or weeks, sit down together. Review what's working well and what isn't. Listen without defensiveness when flaws are pointed out. Take responsibility and understand each other's perspectives. Learn to improve communication, gestures of love, and mutual support.

A Covenantal Relationship is a solemn promise to work together for mutual flourishing. Unlike transactional contracts, covenants are personal and transformative. They require both partners to give their all, aiming for 100% commitment.

While challenging, practicing these principles can dramatically improve your life with God's guidance.

9) Accomplishment

Ultimately, this journey leads to the success of your marriage and family life. Achieving a fulfilling marriage requires both partners to understand themselves and each other deeply. It's crucial to grasp God's purpose for your marriage, as reflected in the vows exchanged: "Until death do us part." Without this clarity, marriages risk failure.

Further Conversations

1. **Awareness:**

   - What does it mean to be aware of challenges within a marriage or family dynamic?

   - How can increased awareness contribute to the healing and wholeness process?

2. **Acknowledgment:**

   - Why is it important to acknowledge issues or conflicts within a marriage or family?

   - What are some strategies for effectively acknowledging these issues?

3. **Admission:**

   - What role does admission of personal responsibility play in the healing process?

   - How can individuals or families navigate admitting mistakes or shortcomings without blame or guilt?

4. **Acceptance:**

    - How does acceptance of differences contribute to family healing?

    - What are some ways to cultivate acceptance within a marriage or family unit?

5. **Adaptation:**

    - Why is adaptation crucial for fostering resilience within families?

    - Can you provide examples of adaptive behaviors or strategies within a family context?

6. **Accommodation:**

    - How does accommodation facilitate understanding in relationships?

    - What are some potential challenges associated with accommodation, and how can they be addressed?

7. **Adjustment:**

    - What distinguishes adjustment from accommodation in the context of family dynamics?

- How can individuals or families navigate periods of significant adjustment effectively?

8. **Assimilation/Acculturation:**

    - How do assimilation and acculturation impact family dynamics, particularly in multicultural and diverse backgrounds?

    - What are some potential benefits and challenges associated with assimilation and acculturation within families?

9. **Assessment:**

    - Why is ongoing assessment important for maintaining family health and well-being?

    - What are some effective strategies for assessing the current state of a marriage or family dynamic?

10. **Accomplishment:**

    - How does celebrating accomplishments contribute to family cohesion and resilience?

    - Can you provide examples of accomplishments within a family context and their significance?

Biblical Covenant Definition

The term *"covenant"* originates from Latin (con venire), meaning a coming together, implying that two or more parties join to form a contract agreeing on promises, stipulations, privileges, and responsibilities. There hasn't been a consensus on the exact meaning of this biblical term in religious and theological contexts, as it is variably used across different biblical passages. In political contexts, it can be likened to a treaty; in social settings, it signifies a lifelong friendship agreement; and in personal relationships, it refers to marriage.

The Evangelical Christian Church in Canada defines the Biblical Covenant:

"The simplest and most straightforward answer is that it's a promise. However, it's not a casual 'if it's convenient, it'll happen' type of promise, but rather an 'I'm going to do whatever it takes to make this happen' type of promise. A covenant is a unilateral promise made for the benefit of someone else. It is not a mutual agreement for mutual benefit; instead, it's a choice made to benefit others or a group of individuals, without concern for personal gain."

In its biblical usage, the term *"covenant"* serves two primary functions:

A Covenant Between God and Man

For example, God covenanted (or promised) with Noah after the flood, ensuring such a judgment would not recur. This is not precisely a covenant between mankind but a promise or agreement by God. The principal covenants are the Covenant of works—God promising salvation and blessings conditioned on perfect obedience—and the Covenant of grace, where God promises salvation to those who believe in Christ and accept Him as Master and Savior. The former is known as the Old Covenant, forming the Old Testament, and the latter as the New Covenant, or New Testament. The Old Covenant, established by God with Adam, Noah, Abraham, Moses, and David, was between God and mankind. As no one greater than God acted as a third-party witness, God swore by Himself, stating, *"I swear by myself, declares the Lord"* (Genesis 22:16).

The Covenant Between Man and Man

This involves a solemn agreement or pact, whether between tribes or nations (Joshua 9:6, 9:15; 1 Samuel 11:1) or individuals (Genesis 31:44), where each party commits to fulfilling certain conditions and expects certain benefits. In making such a covenant, God was invoked solemnly as a witness (Genesis 31:50), and oaths were sworn (Genesis 21:31). Sometimes, a sign or witness of the Covenant was established, such as a gift (Genesis 21:30) or a pillar or heap of stones erected (Genesis 31:52).[12]

---

[12]www.Christianity.com. Bible Definition of Covenant

The Marriage Covenant Grid

At the heart of a strong and lasting marriage lies the concept of Agape Love, a selfless, unconditional love that transcends personal desires and circumstances. Agape Love serves as the foundation of the marriage covenant, emphasizing the importance of genuine care, compassion, and unwavering commitment between partners.

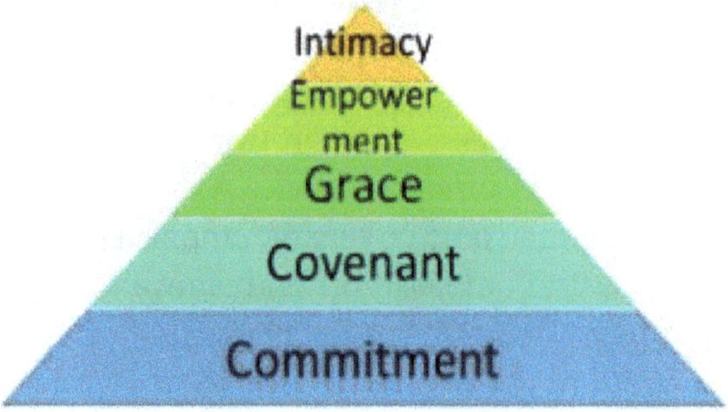
Intimacy
Empowerment
Grace
Covenant
Commitment

Marriage Foundation - Agape Love

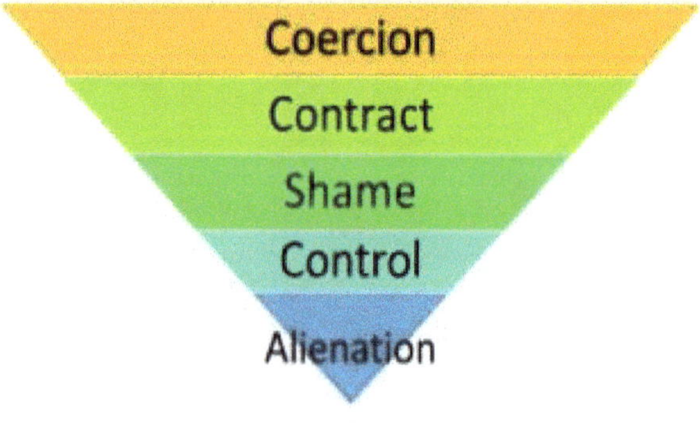
Coercion
Contract
Shame
Control
Alienation

Further Conversations

Commitment. Covenant. Grace. Empowerment. Intimacy

1. Define the Marital Covenant Grid and explain its purpose in evaluating marital relationships. How does it differ from what you have seen or experienced before?

2. Examine the components of the Marital Covenant Grid, including the dimensions of commitment, Covenant, grace, empowerment, and intimacy. How do these dimensions interact to form the foundation of a healthy and fulfilling marriage?

3. Discuss the significance of commitment in the Marital Covenant Grid. What does commitment entail within the context of marriage, and how can you measure your level of commitment, or can it be measured?

4. Intimacy in a marital relationship is more than physical bareness or sexual satisfaction. It's about vulnerability and authenticity. How do emotional, spiritual, and physical intimacy contribute to a strong and resilient marriage?

5. Examine the dimension of grace in the Marital Covenant Grid. How does grace manifest in different aspects of marital life, and how can couples practice grace over time without it becoming static?

6. Discuss the interplay between the dimensions of commitment, grace, and intimacy in the Marital Covenant Grid.

How do changes in one dimension affect the others, and how can couples balance these dimensions to enhance their relationship?

7. What does it mean to empower or be empowered in a marriage relationship? How do cultural norms, gender roles, and religious beliefs shape individuals' perceptions of commitment, Covenant, grace, empowerment, and intimacy within a marriage relationship? What does it look like to empower or be empowered?

8. Examine the role of communication and conflict resolution in strengthening marital relationships. How do effective communication skills contribute to each dimension of the Marital Covenant Grid?

9. Reflect on your own understanding of commitment, Covenant, grace, empowerment, and intimacy in the context of marriage. How do these dimensions align with your personal values and beliefs about marital relationships?

Coercion. Contract. Shame. Control. Alienation

1. **Coercion:**

    - What is coercion, and how does it differ from persuasion or influence?

    - Can coercion be justified in your marriage relationship? Why or why not?

    - How does coercion impact individual autonomy, decision-making, and collaboration?

2. **Contract:**

    - Is a marriage relationship a contract or Covenant? Why is a contract in a marriage relationship not healthy?

    - How do contracts establish rights, responsibilities, and expectations in a marriage relationship?

3. **Shame:**

    - What is shame, and how does it differ from guilt?

    - How can shame be used as a tool for social control or conformity?

- Discuss the psychological effects of shame in a marriage relationship and its potential long-term consequences. In your marriage relationship, have you experienced shame or being shamed? Why?

4. **Control:**

    - How is the control exerted in a marriage relationship? Please explain.

    - What are the mechanisms of control, and how do they affect a marriage relationship?

    - Is there a need for control in a marriage relationship, and why?

5. **Alienation:**

    - What does it mean to be alienated from your marriage, family, and social contexts?

    - How does alienation contribute to feelings of disconnection and estrangement?

    - Discuss the role of alienation in shaping marital, social structures, and power dynamics.

6. **Integration:**

    - How do coercion, contract, shame, control, and alienation intersect in interpersonal, social, and cultural norms?

    - Provide examples of how these concepts can reinforce or challenge each other within specific contexts.

7. **Application:**

    - Reflect on instances where coercion, contract, shame, control, or alienation have influenced your behavior or decisions. What were the outcomes, and how did you navigate them?

    - In what ways can individuals or couples mitigate the negative effects of coercion, shame, control, and alienation while upholding necessary structures and boundaries?

Let's start with insights from Scripture. The Bible begins with the statement, *"In the beginning, God created..."* (Genesis 1:1), marking the origin of time itself. Before God's creation, only eternity existed. When God initiated creation, He introduced time and space alongside the heavens and the earth.

God's creative power is expressed through His spoken word: *"And God said, 'Let there be...' and it was."* This underscores that God's word is authoritative and unchanging. His words are not idle; they are law, reflecting His perfect nature (Psalms 12:6, 18:30; Proverbs 30:5). Jesus affirmed the enduring nature of God's word, stating that while heaven and earth will pass away, His words will never fail (Matthew 24:35; Mark 13:31; Luke 21:33). This highlights the steadfastness and reliability of God's promises—an essential truth for us to grasp.

God created the heavens and the earth, culminating in His creation of man and woman. He blessed them and commanded them to be fruitful and multiply, fill the earth, and subdue it. God's purpose was for us to be good stewards of all His creations and to propagate them. This was a noble task. God deemed humanity worthy of taking on this responsibility, and so He commanded them to do so. Any responsibility we have from Him should be considered a privilege instead of a burden. Our relationship with Him should propel us to take our responsibilities lovingly and without compulsion. Without our love and appreciation for Him and what He has done for us, what we are commanded to do would be a burden too heavy to bear.

After the creation of man and woman and their command to rule over the earth and subdue it, they failed to follow through on God's command. Instead, they believed Satan's subtle and seductive lies and ate the forbidden fruit, which resulted in their death and the death of their posterity for generations. As a result of their disobedience, the whole world was affected. But even after this tragic event, God did not abandon them. He came and provided garments made from sheepskins for them, indicating that animal life would be sacrificed.

He continued to watch over them and their descendants, even after placing flaming angels to guard the gate to Eden. Fast-forwarding, God called Abram out of Ur of the Chaldeans to be a blessing to the world. He commanded him that He would bless him, and he would, in turn, be a blessing to the world. Whoever blesses him will be blessed, and whoever curses him will be cursed. Thus began the Covenant—the Covenant between God and humanity. Through Abram, who is the Father of those who believe, God's Covenant continued and remained binding. Time and again, God's people turned their backs on Him, but He always came through when they cried out for rescue. All of this points back to God's eternal Covenant with Abram. Further back to the creation of the world and the aftermath of the flood, God had promised Himself that as long as He lives, He would not destroy the world as He did in the flood.

What is a *"Covenant?"* According to the dictionary, a covenant is a "sealed contract" agreed upon by two or more parties. However, according to Scripture, a covenant is more than just a written promise. It is initiated by the party that holds more power and authority in the covenantal process. In Scripture, God took the initiative to establish a covenant with Abraham. He did this through the act of circumcision, which He commanded Abraham to undergo.

But before the Covenant, there was a commitment. As Scripture teaches us, prior to making a covenant with Abram, God had committed to redeem humanity. This commitment is evident throughout the Bible, both explicitly and implicitly. For instance, when Adam and Eve realized their nakedness and attempted to cover themselves with fig leaves, God intervened by replacing their inadequate covering with garments made from sheepskin. This act demonstrated God's commitment to humanity. Scripture affirms that God's patience should not be mistaken for slowness in taking action; rather, He desires that none should perish but that all should come to repentance (2 Peter 3:9). Despite His power, which could have allowed Him to start over with new creations after Adam and Eve's disobedience, God chose instead to initiate redemption and establish a covenant with them. This is the character of our God.

Ultimately, in any relationship, it's crucial to distinguish between principles and preferences. The fundamental question to ask is, *"What truly matters in life? What are the core principles I am unwavering on?"* Once we answer these questions clearly, we can avoid conflicts and divisions over trivial, non-essential matters that can harm our relationships.

While I generally hold reservations about CNBC and most media outlets regarding moral and social issues, it's intriguing and somewhat validating to find support for my observations in this context. According to an article and survey by Forbes Advisor, *"There are various reasons why people choose to file for divorce: lack of family support, infidelity, and compatibility rank as the top three."* The survey, which polled 1,000 divorced or divorcing Americans, reveals that nearly all participants believed their marriage could have been saved under different circumstances. Only 5% of respondents felt that nothing could have salvaged their relationship.

Here are the top five factors that divorcees believe could have saved their marriage:

1. A better understanding of the commitment to marriage before marrying
2. A better understanding of the values and morals of their partner before marrying
3. Waiting longer to start a family
4. Seeking professional help from a therapist or couples counselor

5. Waiting longer to get married

In another survey highlighted by Forbes Magazine, 63% of respondents believed that a better understanding of the commitment of marriage before tying the knot could have preserved their relationships.

The survey posed the question: *"But why do so many marriages fail? And why do they tend to fail so early?"* According to the Forbes survey, lack of family support was cited by 43% of respondents as a primary reason for divorce. Thirty-four percent attributed their divorce to infidelity, while 31% cited issues related to incompatibility. Additionally, 31% of respondents mentioned experiencing a lack of intimacy, and an equal percentage noted excessive conflict or arguments. Interestingly, only 24% of respondents identified financial stress as a contributing factor.[13]

Even in society at large, financial issues are not widely seen as a major cause of marriage breakdown. The core issue often lies in a lack of a clear understanding of life's foundational principles and the commitments of marriage. Many marriages that end in divorce typically do not last beyond three years, primarily because one or both spouses come to feel they were deceived or trapped in an undesirable relationship and simply want to exit. No one can tell them otherwise. People are not willing to give grace to offenders. Several years ago, a woman came to me for marital counseling and said to me: *"Pastor. I do not want to continue this relationship with 'this man' (her husband) unless he's been filtered through the ground. If the ground does not filter him, he would not change."*

Ultimately, it boils down to our inability to thoroughly contemplate and discuss the fundamental principles of marriage and life. Many begin their courtship and marriage without fully

---

[13] www.msn.com/en-us/personalfinance/ Why Do Americans Get Divorced? These Are The Top Reasons For Divorce.

understanding the gravity of these principles, although few are willing to admit this oversight. There's a common assumption that simply feeling a deep connection upon first meeting guarantees a smooth journey ahead. However, as the saying goes, *"Time heals all wounds."* In reality, once two people become husband and wife, they often find that the longer they live together, the wider the gap in their relationship can grow. This can lead to deeper and more painful hurts inflicted on each other, whether deliberately or unintentionally.

The Fundamental Principles that Must Not and Will Not Be Crossed

A principle is defined as *"the fundamental truth or position that serves as the foundation for a system of beliefs guiding one's behavior and actions."* For Christians, there are essential principles that govern both life and practice:

The Existence of God and The Creation of the Universe

Ultimately, all human beings believe in one of two possibilities—either there is a God or gods beyond human reach, known as Theists, or there is no god, known as atheists. Theists believe in the existence of powerful deities, while atheists hold that human existence is a result of chance or evolution.

The Creation of Man and The Effects of Sin on Human Life and Relationships

Another fundamental principle for Christians is the belief that God created humanity, who then violated His commandments and sinned. This disobedience severed their relationship with God and impacted their relationships with each other.

Man's Search for Meaning and Purpose

Since then, humans have sought meaning and purpose. King Solomon eloquently expressed this quest in Ecclesiastes. Despite being the wealthiest and wisest man, Solomon concluded that life without God is futile—a chasing after the wind (Ecclesiastes 1:17). Throughout history, humans have pursued meaning through various spiritual quests, often worshipping idols of wood, stone, the moon, or stars, believing them to be gods.

God's Grace and Mercy Toward Sinful Humanity

Scripture teaches that when Adam and Eve disobeyed God by eating from the Tree of the Knowledge of Good and Evil, they introduced sin into humanity, leading to death. Despite this, God's love endures eternally. Initially, God showed His love by providing sheepskin clothing for Adam and Eve to cover their nakedness. Throughout history, God has displayed His grace amidst human corruption, such as through Noah and the construction of the Ark (Genesis 6-8).

Then, God called a man to leave his family, people, and country to go where God would show him. God did this so that he would be a blessing to the world (Genesis 12:1-3).

The pertinent question for today is this: Has God called me out from my family and community to receive blessings and to bless the world? Do I acknowledge this calling in my life, and do I live in a way that allows me to be a blessing to those around me? God could have chosen to impact and transform the world without our involvement, yet out of His eternal love, He has selected us to be His instruments of love and grace to the world.

God's Redemption of Lost Humanity

This foundational principle offers hope and peace. How we perceive our current state influences our interactions and relationships. Our worldview shapes our actions and reactions. Viewing the world solely through our limited human perspective may lead us to prioritize ourselves above others. Believing we are alone and insignificant, we might strive for control, asserting, *"The buck stops with me."*

Conversely, with a worldview that acknowledges I am not the center but that there is a God who loves the world and has a plan to redeem both the world and humanity, I can live with peace and hope.

Jesus Christ is The Redeemer of Lost Humanity

Another crucial principle to grasp is that Jesus Christ is the sole Redeemer of humanity. All people have sinned and fallen short of God's glory. The consequence of sin is death, but God offers the gift of eternal life through Jesus Christ our Lord (Romans 3:23; 6:23).

Our Response to The Message of the Gospel Determines our Final Destiny

Scripture abundantly demonstrates how our response to the gospel message dictates our ultimate destination. Jesus proclaimed, *"For God so loved the world that he gave his one and only Son, that whoever believes in him shall not perish but have eternal life"* (John 3:16). Paul affirms, *"If you confess with your mouth that Jesus is Lord and believe in your heart that God raised him from the dead, you will be saved"* (Romans 10:9). These and other scriptures assure us of God's love through Christ. Eternal life in Christ is not earned; it is a gift freely given by God. Our response is simply to believe and accept this gift by faith.

Without a guiding truth, our actions would clash due to our flawed characters and the changing world around us. It's vital to understand life's core principles, have the moral strength to follow them, and live with integrity.

Love

God calls us to love. We love each other because He first loved us in the first place. Demonstrating love is how we follow Jesus' example and obey His command: *"Love one another as I have loved you."* It's important to grasp the genuine meaning of love, which has often been diluted. The apostle Paul offers a clear definition: *"Love is patient, kind, humble, truthful, and protective"* (1 Corinthians 13:4-7).

Peace

Scripture calls us to peace, naming Jesus the Prince of Peace. Even before His birth, God foretold His role through the Prophet Isaiah: *"For to us a child is born, to us a son is given, and the government will be on his shoulders. And he will be called Wonderful Counselor, Mighty God, Everlasting Father, Prince of Peace"* (Isaiah 9:6-7).

In the New Testament, Jesus declared His mission: *"to preach good news to the poor, to proclaim freedom for the prisoners and recovery of sight for the blind, to release the oppressed, to proclaim the year of the Lord's favor"* (Luke 4:18-19). He assured us that while we will face troubles in the world, in Him, we will find peace. He gives us His peace, urging us not to let our hearts be troubled or afraid. Despite the challenges of this life, we look forward to eternal hope: *"Believe in God; believe also in me. In my Father's house are many rooms; if it were not so, I would have told you. I am going there to prepare a place for you"* (John 14:1-3).

Jesus acknowledged that trouble will come in this world but assured us of His peace. To be free from trouble is to look beyond our present circumstances, trusting in God's plan: *"Believe in God; believe also in me. In my Father's house are many rooms. If it were not so, would I have told you that I am going to prepare a place for you? And if I go and prepare a place for you, I will come back and take you to be with me that you also may be where I am"* (John 14:1-3). While we will face trials as long as we live, we have an advocate who has ascended into heaven and has paved the way for us, as Scripture assures us: *"No one has seen God except the one who came from heaven."*

Holiness

Scripture calls us to purity because of our identification with Christ. We are urged to discard our old selves and embrace the new, focusing on heavenly things (Ephesians 4:24; Colossians 3:10). The blood of Jesus Christ redeems our new selves, and we strive to emulate His holiness, exemplified by His sacrifice on the cross.

Can we achieve holiness on our own? The resounding answer is no. Sin perpetually lurks, as God warned Cain, ready to ensnare and destroy us. However, we have the Holy Spirit dwelling within us, empowering us. Scripture quotes the Lord God, saying,

> *"If you do what is right, will you not be accepted? But if you do not do what is right, sin is crouching at your door; it desires to have you, but you must rule over it"* (Genesis 4:7).

Sin is depicted as a lurking presence eager to dominate our lives, yet God assures us that we can overcome it. To master sin, we must exercise control over our thoughts and actions, surrendering our wills to God's discipline. Achieving holiness through human effort alone is impossible. It requires responding to the Holy Spirit's guidance and allowing His transformative love to work within us.

Honesty and Honor

Honesty is a foundational trait that God calls us to uphold as followers of Christ. Living a life of honesty and integrity is made possible through the empowering presence of the Holy Spirit, recognizing that all of us have sinned and fallen short of God's glory and that our efforts at righteousness are insufficient. Through the Holy Spirit, we are enabled to live a life that is both honest and honorable.

Honesty extends beyond public conduct; it encompasses integrity, guiding how we behave even when no one is watching. On the other hand, honor is bestowed upon those whose public and private lives align.

Scripture reminds us of the deceitful nature of the heart, which is beyond cure (Jeremiah 17:9). Understanding this truth helps us grasp why we often struggle to do what is right and avoid what is wrong (Romans 7:18-20). It is essential to acknowledge and address our deceitful hearts.

Respect for Self and Others

Respect involves acknowledging the inherent value of both oneself and others. It does not involve pride or elevating oneself above others, nor does it mean putting others above oneself. Instead, respect entails having a balanced view of oneself, seeing oneself through God's eyes, and evaluating oneself accordingly. The Oxford Dictionary defines respect as *"admiring someone or something because of their qualities or achievements."*

In relationships, respecting your partner entails recognizing their significance in your life and valuing their role in your well-being. It's about appreciating them for who they are and what they contribute to your life rather than diminishing their importance.

Marriage and Family Principles

Certain principles must be actively lived out daily for any relationship to flourish and thrive. These principles are encapsulated in the acronym TRUST. Trust is fundamental in life; without it, no one can fully flourish as God intended.

1) Truth

The first principle is truth. *"What is truth?"* you ask. You are not the first nor the only one to ask this question. Pilate asked Jesus this question when Jesus was brought before him for condemnation. According to Scripture, Jesus and Pilate discussed whether Jesus was a king. Jesus responded,

> *"My kingdom is not of this world. If it were, my servants would fight to prevent my arrest by the Jewish leaders. But now my kingdom is from another place." "So you are a king then!"* said Pilate. Jesus answered, *"You say that I am a king. In fact, the reason I was born and came into the world is to testify to the truth. Everyone on the side of truth listens to me"* (John 18:37-38).

According to Jesus, *"truth"* transcends the here and now and extends beyond the five senses. Embracing truth requires looking beyond the present and understanding that our actions have eternal consequences. Building trust and gaining trust involves speaking the truth and living it first. Scripture teaches us to live truthfully and to speak truthfully in love. The Law came through Moses, but grace and truth came through Jesus Christ, who exemplified living and speaking truth.

2) Respect

The second principle of marriage is mutual respect. According to Scripture and practical wisdom, respect is both given and received. Scripture instructs us to honor our parents and the elderly (Leviticus 19). Husbands are esteemed for their wives' character and capabilities (Proverbs 13:13, 31:23). In essence, mutual submission is a demonstration of respect for each other. The New Testament encourages Christian households to live out their faith in Jesus Christ by submitting to one another *"out of reverence for Christ"* (Ephesians 5:21). Furthermore, it directs wives to *"submit to your husbands as you do to the Lord,"* and husbands to *"love their wives as Christ loved the church and gave himself up for her"* (Ephesians 5:22-33).

It is sadly common to hear couples publicly criticize each other, using derogatory language that even children would avoid. Such behavior often stems from a desire to incite jealousy or anger, seek attention from others, or assert dominance. However, this approach unwittingly undermines oneself. The underlying motivation may be to diminish others to elevate oneself or assert control in a situation. Yet, the consequence is self-degradation and shame. While attempting to demean others, individuals unknowingly diminish their own dignity and honor.

3) Understanding

The third principle is understanding. True understanding requires actively listening while the other person speaks. Listening goes beyond merely hearing their words; it involves grasping the deeper meaning behind what they are saying. Essentially, understanding entails not only comprehending the content of their message but also appreciating the context in which it is communicated.

Failure to listen attentively results in an incomplete understanding of both the message and its context. Persistent misunderstandings deepen arguments, widen relational gaps, and foster alienation between individuals. In such situations, reconciliation becomes increasingly challenging because neither party is willing to empathize and understand the other's perspective.

4) Support

The fourth principle is support, synonymous with empathy. Supporting our spouse involves empathizing with them, stepping into their shoes, and actively listening to their words, tone of voice, emotions, and body language instead of offering quick answers. True support requires seeing life from their perspective, pausing to pay attention, and allowing them to fully express their thoughts and feelings.

A common challenge is responding rather than reacting. Responding involves intentional pauses and reflections, whereas reacting tends to be spontaneous and defensive. Many of us instinctively become defensive when our spouse speaks, anticipating criticism or needing to justify our actions. This defensive stance often prevents us from genuinely hearing and understanding their perspective.

How often do we find ourselves answering our spouse rather than truly responding? Our unconscious mind may rush to defend ourselves, ready to justify our actions, before fully hearing their concerns. This reflexive need to defend ourselves can overshadow our ability to affirm and validate their feelings and perspectives. In our haste to self-defend, we inadvertently diminish our spouse's voice and feelings, causing unintended harm instead of providing the support they need.

5) Transparency

The final principle of a thriving marriage is transparency. Transparency requires deliberate effort to openly discuss and address aspects of our lives that may affect our relationship. Firstly, it involves acknowledging our respective upbringings, which shape our cultural perspectives and expectations, even if we share the same ethnic background. Our family dynamics and cultural backgrounds significantly influence how we perceive life and relationships.

Secondly, transparency entails being honest about our past relationships before marriage. Previous romantic involvements may have ended on less than positive terms, impacting our ability to be open and vulnerable with each other. Despite these challenges, transparency is essential for fostering genuine connections in marriage.

When building trust, it's crucial to examine our motives. Are we genuinely committed to creating a trustworthy environment, or are there aspects of our lives that we hesitate to disclose? While honesty is crucial, addressing any lingering issues is equally important for cultivating an authentic relationship.

The Bible teaches us that claiming to be without sin deceives us, indicating that truth is not within us (Romans 2:23; 1 John 1:9-10). By embracing honesty and addressing our shortcomings, we build a foundation of trust and authenticity in our marriage. To build trust, it's essential to THINK clearly before we speak. This means carefully considering our intentions, the words we use, and the tone of our voice. Even with good intentions, the way we speak—our tone and choice of words—can profoundly impact the listener, often more than we realize. So what does THINK mean?

Here, again, are the acronyms for THINK:

T - Is it True?

Often, in our conversations, we find ourselves being argumentative and accusatory. We tend to point fingers and defend ourselves, whether or not what the other person says is true. These behaviors can turn discussions into arguments and lead to defensive reactions. Small issues can escalate into serious problems that threaten the marriage.

However, if both spouses focus on honest communication and are willing to accept constructive criticism—even if it hurts their pride—they can grow personally and strengthen their roles as spouses and parents. Similarly, speaking truthfully and lovingly to your partner can help them develop their character.

H - Is it Honoring?

Respect is essential in marriage. From my years of counseling couples, I've seen how belittling each other, whether in private or in public, can harm relationships in the long term. Dishonoring your spouse won't humble them or lead to submission; instead, it damages both them and the relationship.

It's crucial to honor your spouse as an equal partner in your marriage journey. While some people may be difficult to respect, we are reminded in Romans 12:10 to *"honor one another above yourselves."* Therefore, we should strive to treat each other with respect in all our interactions and conversations, as this is a key aspect of being a Christ follower.

I - Is it Instructive?

Intentional instructiveness is crucial in our communication with each other, whether we are speaking or listening. In an ideal world, one might think that their spouse is the easiest person to instruct. However, we must recognize that our reality is far from ideal. In fact, some of the most challenging individuals to instruct can be our spouses and immediate family members (John 4:44).

When we talk about being *"instructive,"* the focus is on the speaker: What is the main point you want to convey? What do you want your listener to understand without repeating yourself excessively or laboring the point? How can you communicate truths without seeming to criticize your spouse's attitudes or actions?

The challenge lies in carefully considering the content of our words and ensuring they are instructive to our spouse. What do you hope your spouse will take away from this conversation? How can you communicate effectively so that your spouse does not feel criticized? These questions are crucial to reflect on when communicating with your spouse.

N - Is it Nice and Non-accusative?

Being nice isn't always easy, especially in long-term relationships where familiarity can lead us to think we know our spouse thoroughly, often overlooking areas where deeper understanding is needed. Due to this familiarity, we might unintentionally expect them to read our minds during communication, which can sometimes come across as accusatory in both our words and tone. Many of our heated conversations stem from pointing fingers or putting up walls where we blame or defend ourselves.

In these moments, none of us are innocent of accusations or defensiveness. Instead of blaming or becoming defensive, we should be mindful of both our and our partner's perspectives, allowing freedom and growth in marital conversations. Often, our desire not to be seen as the villain or to avoid blame leads us to justify our behavior by saying, *"This is just who I am. Take it or leave it."*

Yet, by refusing to acknowledge our shortcomings and strive for kindness, we eliminate room for mistakes and, consequently, for grace on both sides.

K - Is it Kind?

Kindness originates from the heart, which we often refer to as more than just a physical organ but as the core of our being. It embodies an essential part of one's character. Throughout Scripture, kindness is prominently featured: from God's kindness towards humanity, such as covering Adam and Eve after their sin in the Garden of Eden (Genesis 3), to God's grace towards Noah by instructing him to build an ark (Genesis 6), and God's call to Abram (Genesis 12). Even Joseph showed his brothers kindness during the Canaan famine (Genesis 37-41). Kindness, in a sense, is not just not retaliate against wrongs, but goes the extra mile, taking the extra effort to protect the vulnerable and provide for the needy.

Scripture consistently underscores kindness as integral to love, affirming that *"love is kind."* Kindness naturally flows from a loving heart. The words we speak to our spouse can either carry kindness or harshness; our tone can be gentle or sharp. How we communicate profoundly impacts our partner and others, depending on how we deliver our message. This doesn't mean diluting the truth but rather speaking it with love from a compassionate heart to our beloved, packaged with kindness.

In showing kindness to each other, we reflect the kindness of the Lord towards us, echoing our creation in His image—the *"imago Dei."*

Further Conversations

Truth:

- What is the significance of truth in personal, marital, and family relationships?

- How does embracing truthfulness contribute to building trust and credibility?

- Is truth subjective? Who determines truth—individuals, culture, or society? Why or why not?

Respect:

- Why is respect important in interpersonal communication and collaboration?

- How can one demonstrate respect towards their spouse and extended family members?

- What are the consequences of lacking respect in marital and family relationships?

Understanding:

- What role does empathy play in fostering understanding between individuals or groups?

- How can active listening enhance one's ability to understand others' perspectives?

- Discuss the significance of seeking to understand before seeking to be understood.

Support:

- In what ways can emotional support impact individuals during challenging times?

- How does providing support contribute to building strong relationships and communities?

- Can support sometimes be detrimental? How do we ensure support is empowering rather than enabling?

Transparency:

- Why is transparency important in marital relationships?

- What are the ethical implications of withholding information or being opaque?

- How can transparency be balanced with the need for privacy and confidentiality?

Integration:

- How do truth, respect, understanding, support, and transparency intersect in building healthy relationships and fostering effective communication?

- Provide examples of situations where these values conflict. How can such conflicts be resolved while upholding each value?

Application:

- Reflect on personal experiences where truth, respect, understanding, support, or transparency played a significant role. What did you learn from these experiences?

- In what ways can individuals or couples actively cultivate these values in their daily interactions and decision-making processes to enhance their flourishing?

Preference and Principles in Marital Relationships

Preference is defined as favoring something or someone over another, reflecting personal choice or specific tastes. In many marriages, personal preferences often overshadow foundational life principles. The breakdown of marriages frequently arises not from moral failings but from trivial misunderstandings and miscommunications rooted in differing personal preferences between partners. Small issues like how the toilet paper is placed or how toothpaste is squeezed can escalate into conflicts and tensions.

To minimize such conflicts, couples must address these differences proactively. First, spouses need to distinguish between personal preferences and agreed-upon principles in their marriage. What foundational truths guide their relationship? Engaging in serious conversations about these non-negotiable principles is essential.

Secondly, acknowledging personal preferences is important. These preferences can hinder relationship growth and maturity. Recognizing our own shortcomings and committing to improvement can help us gradually loosen our grip on personal preferences. This willingness fosters relationship growth, tranquility, and deeper mutual affection.

Thirdly, as we become more aware and openly acknowledge our biases, we develop the capacity to accept our spouse's imperfections without undue emotional turmoil. Acceptance is the first step toward letting go of personal preferences, symbolizing growth and maturation in our thoughts and actions.

Another indicator of maturity, moving from preferences to principles, is the ability to constructively address our spouse's shortcomings without fear of being overly critical or offensive. This confidence to speak truth in love echoes the wisdom of Scripture. This progression mirrors the developmental journey described by the Apostle Paul in 1 Corinthians 13:11, comparing the growth from childhood to adulthood and emphasizing personal and relational maturity.

As we mature physically, we experience emotional, mental, and social growth. We learn to differentiate between principles—values we hold dear—and preferences—individual likes and dislikes. Mature adults recognize that what they value may not align with their partner's preferences. Understanding and living by principles contribute to maturity in terms of reasoning and behavior, marking a departure from childish ways of thinking.

Further Conversations

1. Define the concepts of principles and personal preferences in the context of marriage. How do they influence decision-making and behavior within a marital relationship?

2. Provide examples of principles in marriage, such as mutual respect, trust, and commitment. How do these principles serve as foundational elements for a healthy and fulfilling relationship?

3. Discuss the distinction between principles that are universally valued across cultures and personal preferences that may vary among individuals. How can couples navigate differences in preferences while upholding shared principles in their marriage?

4. In a marriage relationship, is there such a thing as compromise and negotiation in reconciling conflicting principles and personal preferences? What does that look like? How can couples find a balance between honoring each other's values and maintaining their own integrity?

5. Reflect on your own values and beliefs about marriage. Identify which aspects are based on timeless principles and which are influenced by personal preferences or cultural norms. How do these factors shape your expectations and behavior in relationships?

6. Discuss the potential challenges that arise when personal preferences conflict with established principles in marriage. How

can couples navigate these challenges while preserving the integrity of their relationship?

7. Examine the importance of communication and mutual understanding in clarifying principles and personal preferences within a marital relationship. How can open dialogue facilitate compromise and strengthen the bond between partners?

8. Over time, principles can shift and fade into the background if not consciously guarded. Discuss how principles can be maintained without becoming overly rigid or irrelevant.

9. Reflect on the concept of growth and change in marriage. How might individuals' principles and personal preferences evolve over time, and how can couples adapt to these changes while maintaining a strong foundation for their relationship?

10. Discuss the role of shared values and goals in aligning principles and personal preferences within a marital partnership. How can couples cultivate common ground while respecting each other's opinions and perspectives?

11. Reflect on the differences between foundational principles that a couple should live by and functional preferences they want to live with. How do these differences practically affect their relationship and potential growth?

Practicing Our Principles Instead of Functioning Out of Our Personal Preferences

The key to minimizing marital conflict is understanding our values. Many people assume they know their values, but when asked to articulate them, they often struggle. Values are core principles and the unbreakable foundations that define us. When we marry, we may assume our partner shares our values, but this isn't automatically the case. Each partner brings their own values into the relationship, and these need to be understood by both.

First, we must understand and clearly articulate our principles to ourselves and our partner. This requires time and effort to reflect on what we truly value instead of what we simply prefer. Values are distinct from preferences. If we can't express our values clearly, it will be difficult for our partner to understand them. Communication, I've learned, is inherently challenging and requires skill from both the speaker and the listener. Cultural, language and educational differences can make this even more complex.

Second, ensuring that both partners align on their values is essential. This means taking the time to understand and accept each other's core principles as significant. When both partners are on the same page, they share a common vision and direction for their relationship. This mutual understanding allows the couple to work towards the same goals, helping them to thrive and flourish together. This alignment benefits not only the couple but also their future generations.

Patience

Patience means being able to wait without becoming frustrated or angry. The Bible describes patience as not being easily angered, highlighting that the effort and intentionality behind waiting are what truly matter. Love and patience are inseparable; love is inherently patient, and patience is an expression of love. Without patience, there can be no genuine love, and vice versa. This might seem simple, but it's profoundly true. Practicing patience demands patience itself, much like how practicing discipline requires discipline. While it may seem paradoxical, it makes sense when you think about it.

Kindness

Kindness is often praised as a virtue but can be difficult to implement. True kindness means accommodating others, even when they act selfishly or rudely. Our level of kindness is shown by how much we can tolerate unreasonable behavior without feeling entitled to better treatment. However, being kind does not mean allowing others to mistreat us or walk all over us. It involves balancing compassion for others with maintaining our own dignity and self-respect.

Humility

Many conflicts in relationships stem from personal preferences and pride rather than clear-cut issues of right and wrong. Often, our pride is driven by fear—the fear of *"losing face"* and the deeper fear of exposing our true selves. The Bible offers wisdom on this: *"Wisdom's instruction is to fear the Lord, and humility comes before honor. Before a downfall, the heart is haughty. But humility comes before honor"* (Proverbs 15:33; 18:12).

These verses teach that pride leads to downfall while humility precedes honor. Those who fear God stay humble because they understand it is wise. They recognize that they are not God and are powerless on their own, whereas God is the author of life. Pride achieves nothing and ultimately destroys the proud person. In contrast, the humble, who submit to God, receive grace and are lifted up in due time. When God decides to elevate the humble, He grants them honor. Therefore, Scripture advises that anyone seeking honor should learn to humble themselves before God and others.

Pride may seem to protect the proud person from harm initially, but it ultimately leads to their downfall. Proverbs 16:18 warns, *"Pride goes before destruction, a haughty spirit before a fall"* (NIV). This means that pride sets the stage for one's eventual ruin.

A similar message is conveyed in the New Testament:

> *"In the same way, you who are younger, submit yourselves to your elders. All of you clothe yourselves with humility toward one another because 'God opposes the proud but shows favor to the humble.' Therefore, humble yourselves under God's mighty hand so that he may lift you up in due time. Cast all your anxiety on him because he cares for you"* (1 Peter 5:5-7, NIV).

> *"Be alert and of sober mind. Your enemy, the devil, prowls around like a roaring lion, looking for someone to devour. Resist him, standing firm in the faith, because you know that the family of believers throughout the world is undergoing the same kind of suffering"* (1 Peter 5:5-9).

Speaking through Peter, the Holy Spirit instructs us to submit to one another and clothe ourselves with humility. But what does it mean to be *"clothed with humility"*? True humility might seem intangible and out of reach. If humility were inherent within us, we wouldn't need to *"put it on"* or be *"clothed"* with it. This suggests that humility is something given to us, which we must actively choose to wear for it to manifest in our lives. Putting on humility requires active participation; we cannot passively hope for it to develop on its own.

The challenge with humility often stems from pride, which is essentially a form of fear. Pride acts as a front, but behind it lies the fear of being exposed or having our weaknesses discovered.

Another important principle to remember and practice is that our humility is not just about our relationships with others but also about our relationship with God. We must humble ourselves under God's mighty hand, for He is all-powerful and capable of upholding and sustaining us. One reason it's difficult to humble ourselves is because we are often anxious. Scripture reassures us that we can cast our anxiety on Him because He cares for us. This is both refreshing and liberating.

Holding onto anxiety is challenging because we want to control our feelings and attitudes. However, do you realize that clinging to anxiety only keeps us anxious? Anxiety is like a prison cell, where negative thoughts and behaviors hold us captive. We cannot control our fears on our own, so we need to let go and lay them before the Lord. Scripture tells us that God cares for us and wants to free us from our fears and anxieties.

Scripture teaches us that pride and humility have opposing effects on us. Firstly, God's stance towards the proud is clear: *"The Lord opposes the proud."* Pride has no place in the kingdom of God; there is no room for it in heaven. The primary reason Satan was cast out of heaven was his pride. Pride positions itself against everyone, including God Himself.

Forgiveness

"Forgiveness?" What do we mean by *"forgiveness?"* Again, words are important and have meaning. Forgiveness is crucial because it impacts every aspect of our lives profoundly. We might claim to have forgiven those who wronged us, but we haven't truly forgiven unless we grasp the full implications of forgiveness. It's that simple.

Keeping grudges is like a prison cell that continues to hold both the unforgiver and the unforgiven captive. As long as we harbor resentment towards others, we imprison ourselves as well as them. We're all in the same prison, just in different cells.

Forgiveness is crucial in marriage because it liberates us to live the life God intends for us and allows us to pursue the life we desire. But what does forgiveness really mean, and how do we practice it? The Merriam-Webster Dictionary defines *"forgiveness"* as *"an intentional decision, both socially and mentally, to let go of the hurt that results in anger and resentment.*[14]*"* Biblically, forgiveness is defined as letting go of the offender without any demand for payment.[15] Forgiveness has a four-dimensional effect on ourselves - physically, emotionally, socially, and spiritually.

From a mental and psychological standpoint, forgiveness involves releasing oneself from emotional and mental burdens. It's essential for your well-being to forgive those who have wronged you, regardless of the offense.

Letting go of grudges and bitterness can pave the way for better health and inner peace. According to a recent article by the Mayo Clinic staff, practicing forgiveness can lead to:

- Healthier relationships with self and others.
- Improved mental health for self.

---

[14]Merriam-Webster Dictionary define 'Forgiveness' as 'to cease to feel resentment against the offender.

[15]Forgiveness in Scripture, in the Greek, means to literally let go of the debtor without demanding any payment. As Jesus taught his disciples to pray, "Forgive us our sins as we forgive those who sin against us" - Matthew 6:12.

- Less anxiety, stress, and hostility toward self and others.
- Fewer symptoms of depression.
- Lower blood pressure.
- A stronger immune system.
- Improved heart health.
- Improved self-esteem. Increased self-confidence.[16]

From a social perspective, forgiveness grants us the freedom to engage more openly with others, including those who have hurt us. It allows us to reconnect confidently without fear or hesitation.

However, the most profound aspect of forgiveness lies in our spiritual and emotional healing. Jesus emphasizes its importance, saying,

"For if you forgive other people when they sin against you, your heavenly Father will also forgive you. But if you do not forgive others their sins, your Father will not forgive your sins" (Matthew 6:14-15). This underscores that our own forgiveness is intertwined with our ability to forgive others.

Firstly, our connection with God through the Lord Jesus Christ is profound. Scripture teaches us,

"At just the right time, when we were still powerless, Christ died for the ungodly. Very rarely will anyone die for a righteous person, though for a good person, someone might possibly dare to die. But God demonstrates his own love for us in this: While we were still sinners, Christ died for us" (Romans 5:6-8).

Jesus' death on the cross was not random but purposeful, occurring at precisely the appointed time. Despite our ungodliness, His sacrifice has eternal implications for our relationships and ultimate destiny.

---

[16] www.mayoclinic.com Mayo Clinic Adult Health. By Mayo Clinic Staff Online. This source tells us that forgiveness of self and others free us to live healthier and more productive lives. Our perception of others affects our self-image.

Secondly, our connection with others who confess Jesus Christ as Savior and Lord is crucial. Scripture teaches us that Jesus himself is our peace, who has made the two groups one and has destroyed the barrier, the dividing wall of hostility, by setting aside in his flesh the law with its commands and regulations. His purpose was to create in himself one new humanity out of the two, thus making peace, and in one body to reconcile both of them to God through the cross, by which he put to death their hostility. He came and preached peace to you who were far away and peace to those who were near. For through him, we both have access to the Father by one Spirit (Ephesians 2:14-18). *"The most intriguing example of Jesus' presence afffects human relationships is recorded in Luke's Gospel. According to Scripture, the day Herod met Jesus, did not only meet Jesus of whom he had heard so much about, but had been reconciled with Pilate, his enemy"* (Luke 23:12).

In his book *"Soul Care: 7 Transformational Principles for a Healthy Soul,"* Dr. Rob Reimer emphasizes that forgiveness is a deliberate choice made by the forgiver, recognizing that God extends forgiveness through the death and resurrection of Jesus Christ on the cross. Reimer reflects on his own realization that he had sinned against God, but Jesus Christ's sacrifice redeemed him and forgave all his sins.

Inspired by John Maxwell's statement about dying without enemies at a conference, Reimer decided to apply this wisdom in his life. He said, *"I have decided to bless everyone who curses me. I have determined to hold no grudges, nurse no wounds, nurture no disappointment, and hang on to no resentments. I will process my anger and pain at all costs and forgive my enemies. That decision has saved my life countless hours of internal anguish and torment."*[17] Forgiveness is good not just for the offender but also for the offended. You forgive for your own good.

---

[17]Reimer, Robert. Soul Care: 7 Transformational Principles For A Healthy Soul. Franklin, Tennessee: Carpenter's Son Publishing. P. 47.

Acceptance

Acceptance involves recognizing our own presence and the presence of others around us. Our awareness of how our presence affects others can reveal aspects of our personality. Some people naturally exude warmth and hospitality, making others feel welcome. Conversely, others may unintentionally evoke feelings of fear or intimidation in those around them. In such cases, individuals need to learn how to disarm these unconscious tensions and create a more welcoming atmosphere.

Stewardship

Stewardship involves understanding who I am and the resources entrusted to me and living according to this understanding. When I know myself and live accordingly, I can minimize potential regrets in life.

What distinguishes a steward from a servant? The key difference lies in their relationship with the master. A servant serves their master in the hope of earning freedom from servitude. They serve to gain favor with the master in order to be released.

On the other hand, a steward serves their master not to escape from their control but out of reverence, respect, and mutual love.

a) Relationship

God created us as social beings, designed to have relationships with ourselves, others, and with Him. However, due to our first parents' disobedience to God's commands, these relationships have been significantly altered and damaged. Therefore, restoring these relationships poses a significant challenge.

i. **With God:** Who is God to you? This question is fundamental because it defines our existence and guides our daily lives. Jesus taught, *"No one can serve two masters. Either you will hate the one and love the other, or you will be devoted to the one and despise the other. You cannot serve both God and money"* (Matthew 6:24). This challenges us to reflect on whether God is truly our priority, or if we treat Him as a means to get what we want—a belief often revealed in our actions. Do we honor God in practice as we claim to believe in our minds? This is a question that requires deep contemplation.

ii. **With self:** Who am I as an individual (man/woman)? How do others perceive me, and how do I see myself when I look in the mirror? Personal identity is closely tied to how I treat myself. Many of us strive to please others through our actions without considering why we do what we do. However, the apostle Paul reminds us in 1 Corinthians 6:19-20 that our bodies are temples of the Holy Spirit, given to us by God. We are not our own; we belong to God, who purchased us with a price. Therefore, we are called to honor God with our bodies by caring for them—through proper nutrition, rest, and responsible work habits. This understanding underscores the importance of respecting and caring for ourselves as vessels of God's Spirit.

iii. **With spouse/family:** In relation to my family, who am I—a *"king"* or a *"steward, caretaker"*? A king typically rules, whereas a steward serves and cares for others. The role of a king is to command obedience, while a steward prioritizes meeting others' needs with attentiveness and diligence. Jesus beautifully exemplified both roles when He washed His disciples' feet and declared, *"The Son of Man did not come to be served, but to serve, and to give His life as a ransom for many"* (Matthew 20:28; Mark 10:45).

iv. **With others:** How I relate to others reflects my relationship with them. The way I treat others has a significant impact on me spiritually and emotionally. Jesus taught, *"In everything, do to others what you would have them do to you, for this sums up the Law and the Prophets"* (Matthew 7:12). This golden rule emphasizes treating others with the same kindness and respect that I desire for myself. It reminds me that my actions towards others directly reflect how I view and value myself. Scripture commands us to love our neighbors as ourselves (Matthew 22:37-39), highlighting the interconnectedness of our relationships and self-perception.

b) **Time**

i. Where do you spend your time? Your choice of how and where you spend your time reflects your values and priorities. Whether it's at the lake or attending sports games, these activities aren't necessarily wasteful. However, it's important to consider if our time investments align with our personal growth and well-being. Each choice signifies different priorities and impacts our lives in unique ways.

ii. How do you spend your time? How you choose to spend your time directly reflects your values and priorities. Many of us guard our time as a personal possession, believing it's solely our decision how to use it. Whether we decide to sleep all day or engage in unproductive activities, it's seen as our prerogative. However, these choices ultimately shape our lives and define what we prioritize, impacting our personal growth and fulfillment.

iii. What you spend your time on reveals your stewardship of your time. Consider how you allocate your time: Are you investing it in activities like sports or events that enrich your life? Some might view this as meddling, asserting that their time is their own to manage as they see fit. While this is true, it's valuable to seek guidance from God's word. Scripture offers direction on how to use our time wisely and purposefully, urging us to prioritize serving others and living with intentionality within the twenty-four hours given to us each day.

iv.

c) **Treasure**

i. **Where you spend your treasure:** *"Where your treasure is, there your heart will be also."* But what exactly is *"treasure?"* The Merriam-Webster Dictionary defines *"treasure"* as *"valuables"* such as gold, silver, jewelry, and other precious stones. Essentially, treasure is what holds the most value to you. What we set our hearts on indicates what we treasure. Do we spend our resources on exotic vacations and world travel? Our actions and the places where we invest our resources reveal a great deal about our priorities and values.

ii. **How you spend your treasure:** Do you squander it, or do you steward it wisely? The story of the prodigal son that Jesus told, as recorded in Luke 15, comes to mind.

1) First, the younger son asked for something that wasn't his—it belonged to his father. The wealth had been accumulated by his father, not by him. Yet, he behaved as though he deserved it. He demanded, *"Father, give me my share of the estate."* Notice he said, *"Give me my share,"* as if he had contributed to accumulating the estate. He acted entitled to an equal share of what his father had earned.

2) Second, despite the younger son's attitude, his father generously chose to divide his wealth between his two sons.

The younger son said, *"Father, give me my portion of the inheritance,"* acting entitled to his father's wealth. He failed to understand that as long as his father was alive, nothing truly belonged to him—it was all still his father's.

3) Third, the younger son squandered what was given to him because he didn't earn it. He didn't work for or sweat to get his inheritance. He spent recklessly, not understanding the value of the gift or considering that he had no income and no interest accumulating. Eventually, his assets ran out, and his pockets were emptied. As the Hmong saying goes, *"Even rivers can dry up."*

4) Poverty caught up to him, and it was too late. The naive young man found himself in a crisis. Desperate to survive, he hired himself out to a swine owner to feed the pigs. Then, he *"came to his senses"* and realized that even his father's hired men, who worked the fields, were better off than he was. Determined to improve his situation, he decided to return home. He didn't expect to be welcomed back as his father's son but hoped to be hired as a servant just to have the same provisions as his father's workers.

5) Another point about stewardship is the older brother, who seemed to be *"a good boy"* and was faithful and obedient to the task at hand. As we can infer from the story, he had not disobeyed his father's commands. When his younger brother returned home and their father celebrated by butchering the fattened calf, the older brother was furious and indignant. He said to his father, *"All these years I've been slaving for you and never disobeyed your orders. Yet you never gave me even a young goat so I could celebrate with my friends"* (Luke 15:29-30). Notice his words: *"All these years I've been slaving for you and never disobeyed your orders."*

6) What is intriguing is the older son's comments to his father: *"All these years I have been slaving for you and never*

disobeyed your orders." This reveals the older son's mindset. He believes he has been *"slaving"* for his father, implying that he sees his years of hard work as burdensome and unjustly rewarded. Although he has been working *"faithfully,"* he harbors unspoken resentment and grudges against both his younger brother and his father. The older son does not realize that all his father's accumulated wealth will eventually be his inheritance. Everything his father has will ultimately fall into his lap.

7) Here's what his father responds: *"My son, you are always with me, and everything I have is yours"* (v. 31). The older son has forgotten that everything his father has is already his to keep. His father won't live forever, and eventually, all the wealth he has been working for will be inherited by him. This is the essence of stewardship. We may not have everything now, but everything is ours in the future. Our perspective on this reality impacts how we care for what we currently have.

The question remains: What do you think of what you have? And what do you do with what you have been given? Do you squander it or steward it? This choice depends largely on our perception. If we view our possessions and responsibilities as a form of enslavement, we might be inclined to *"spend"* everything we have impulsively and without thought. However, if we view what we have as an opportunity for stewardship, we will cherish and manage it wisely, no matter how much or how little it is. This perspective encourages us to appreciate and take care of our possessions, recognizing their value and potential for good.

d) Talents

In Jesus' parable of the talents, found in Matthew 25:14-28, the master delegates duties and responsibilities to his servants, each according to their abilities. While the master is away, two of the servants wisely invest the talents they receive, while the third buries his talent. When the master returns, he calls them to account for how they have managed what was entrusted to them.

The first two servants in the parable of the talents brought back what they had been given, along with additional earnings (interest or profit). The master commended them, saying,

"Well done, good and faithful servants! You have been faithful with a few things; I will put you in charge of many things."

Then the third servant came forward and proudly presented what he had been given, saying to the master, *"I knew that you are a hard man, harvesting where you have not sown and gathering where you have not scattered seed. So I was afraid and went out and hid your gold in the ground. See, here is what belongs to you."*

His master replied,

"You wicked, lazy servant! So you knew that I harvest where I have not sown and gather where I have not scattered seed? Well then, you should have put my money on deposit with the bankers, so that when I returned, I would have received it back with interest."

It's surprising how this servant responds to his master. His reason for burying the treasure is fear. He said, *"...you are a hard man,"* implying that his master intends to take advantage of others. Due to this assumption, the servant decided not to let the master profit from his labor. Therefore, he did his master a 'favor' by burying what belonged to him.

The point of the story of the talents is clear: each of us has been entrusted with abilities and resources. The crucial question is how we choose to utilize them. Will we squander them or steward them wisely? Just like the servants in the parable, who were expected to invest their talents and generate returns, we, too, are accountable for what we do with what we've been given. Whether we bury or invest our talents wisely, our actions will eventually be evaluated and accounted for.

i. How do you invest your talents? Investment is an economic term. A financial term. Most of us would not understand the meaning of the term unless we paid attention to it. To invest means to take an interest in the means and to focus on it in the long term.

1) The simple answer might be, *"To fulfill Christ's kingdom, of course."* But is it really that simple? It's more challenging than we might think. First, we need to understand what Christ's kingdom entails and how we can actively contribute to fulfilling its purpose. Even before Jesus began his ministry, John the Baptist was preaching to the crowds, urging them to repent, for *"the kingdom of God is at hand"* (Matt. 3:2). When Jesus began his ministry, he echoed the same message, saying, *"Repent, for the kingdom of heaven is at hand"* (Matthew 4:17).

Investing in Christ's kingdom, as Apostle Paul described in Romans 10:14-15, involves critical steps: first, people must hear the gospel, and for that to happen, someone must preach it. Those who support missionaries financially and through prayer are also crucial. Secondly, if one is called to go, then go. This defines stewardship in Christ's kingdom. Another aspect of stewardship is faithfully and consistently sharing the gospel within one's family. Do you share it openly or keep it within, hoping others will see your life and come to believe?

2) For pleasure or profit? Investing our talents reveals our values and character. When we face judgment, our choices in using our talents for pleasure or profit will reflect who we truly are.

ii. Who do you spend your talents with? I've observed people who accumulate wealth but primarily spend it on themselves, for themselves. It's not inherently wrong to indulge in leisure activities or purchase material goods for enjoyment. However, seeking satisfaction and fulfillment solely through excessive self-indulgence is misguided. No amount of wealth can truly satisfy or bring contentment; instead, it often adds burdens and sleepless nights.

Returning to the concept of stewardship, Scripture reminds us that one day, *"Every knee will bow and every tongue confess that Jesus is Lord"* (Philippians 2:11). This moment underscores that each of us will be held accountable for how we have used what we've been given. We must be prepared to give an account when that time comes.

Emotional Intelligence

What has been discussed so far would make little sense if we fail in our emotional intelligence. So what is emotional intelligence? Emotional intelligence is defined as *"the ability to perceive, use, manage, and understand emotions."* People with higher emotional intelligence can perceive and understand their own emotions and those of others. It involves managing our emotions intelligently, so we control our emotions rather than letting our emotions control us. It is the ability to understand your feelings and how they affect you. EQ also involves understanding the feelings of others. It is about how we process delayed gratification, fear, anger, and anxiety. EQ requires self-awareness and awareness of others. People with good self-awareness understand how their emotions affect them and those around them.

Many talk about *"putting yourself in someone else's shoes,"* but it takes mature emotional intelligence to genuinely do so. To understand ourselves and our spouse, we must be aware of and in touch with our emotional state and ask ourselves why we act or react the way we do. Peter Scazzero, in his book Emotionally Healthy Spirituality[18], categorizes our emotions in stages as follows:

Emotional Infants

- **Dependency**: Look for others to take care of them.
- **Empathy**: Have great difficulty entering into the world of others.
- **Instant Gratification**: Are driven by the need for immediate satisfaction.
- **Utilitarian Relationships**: Use others as objects to meet their needs.

---

[18]Emotionally Healthy Spirituality, Peter Scazzero, pp. 178-179. Emotional Intelligence is so important for those who are serious about their own personal growth and well-being and that of those whom they lead to learn and live these truth.

Emotional Children

- **Conditional Happiness**: Are content and happy as long as they get what they want.
- **Temper**: Get angry quickly in the face of stress and disappointments.
- **Personalization**: Interpret disagreements as personal offenses.
- **Sensitivity**: Are easily hurt.
- **Manipulative Behaviors**: Complain, withdraw, manipulate, take revenge, become sarcastic when they don't get their way.
- **Communication**: Have great difficulty calmly discussing their needs and wants in a mature, loving way.

Emotional Adolescents

- **Defensiveness**: Tend to often be defensive.
- **Criticism Sensitivity**: Are threatened and alarmed by criticism.
- **Transactional Relationships**: Keep score of what they give to ask for something later in return.
- **Conflict Avoidance**: Deal with conflict poorly, often blaming, going to a third person, pouting, or ignoring the issue entirely.
- **Self-Centeredness**: Become preoccupied with themselves.
- **Empathy Deficit**: Have great difficulty truly listening to another person's pain or needs.
- **Judgmental Attitude**: Are critical and judgmental.

Emotional Adults

- **Direct Communication**: Can ask for what they need, want, or prefer directly and honestly.
- **Emotional Responsibility**: Recognize, manage, and take responsibility for their thoughts and feelings.
- **Stress Management**: Can, when under stress, state their own beliefs and values without becoming adversarial.
- **Respect for Others**: Respect others without feeling the need to change them.

- **Acceptance**: Give people room to make mistakes and not be perfect.
- **Appreciation**: Appreciate people for who they are – the good, bad, and ugly – not for what they can give back.
- **Empathy**: Are deeply in tune with their emotional world and able to enter into the feelings, needs, and concerns of others without losing themselves.
- **Conflict Resolution**: Have the capacity to resolve conflict maturely and negotiate solutions that consider the perspectives of others.[19]

The question is: Who or what are you? At what stage are you emotionally? Look at the stages of emotional growth and maturity listed above. Are you still a child emotionally? Do you still behave like a child? None of us want to be labeled or called a child, yet many of us continue to behave like children. We unconsciously expect our spouse to take care of us, believing we deserve their services simply because we *"married"* them. When someone suggests that we are behaving childishly, we often react with excitement and anger, which is, ironically, a childish response.

The Apostle Paul was keenly aware of this dynamic. He said,

"When I was a child, I talked like a child, I thought like a child, I reasoned like a child. When I became a man, I put the ways of childhood behind me" (1 Corinthians 13:11).

Putting childish ways behind us means stopping the behavior associated with being a child. The challenge is clear: *"Grow up."*

Another dimension of emotional intelligence is being conscious of our inner selves, especially as followers of Christ. Addressing Christian leadership, Justin A. Irving and Mark L. Strauss, in their

---

[19]Emotionally Healthy Spirituality, Ibid. For a more in depth understanding about this topic, I would recommend the reader explore other resources pertaining to this topic. It is an area that most leadership subjects do not discus and is greatly lacking in leadership endeavors, especially in the local church context.

book *"Leadership in Christian Perspective: Biblical Foundations and Contemporary Practices for Servant Leaders,"* state:

"For Christian leaders, this certainly includes attention to the spiritual dimensions of soul care. But attention to soul care necessarily relates to other areas, such as emotional, financial, physical, vocational, and relational health. Unhealthy self-leadership in any of these areas can have a lasting negative effect on the lives of those we lead."

"Consider how a lack of attention to simple dimensions in one's life can have devastating effects. Some use the acronym HALT to illustrate this: when one is Hungry, Angry, Lonely, or Tired, these states can profoundly impact a person's emotional well-being and decision-making." To this, I might add *"Suffer."*

To summarize Irving and Strauss, how you act and react when you are in a HALTS state tells you and those around you a lot about yourself. It reveals your character and behavior in your roles as a spouse, parent, family member, community member, and, most importantly, as a follower and ambassador for Christ.

Further Conversations

1. Examine the impact of emotional intelligence (EQ) on leadership effectiveness. How do leaders with high EQ skills inspire and motivate others?

2. Explore the relationship between emotional intelligence and interpersonal relationships. How does EQ contribute to effective communication, conflict resolution, and collaboration?

3. Reflect on your own level of emotional intelligence. What are your strengths and areas for improvement? How can you enhance your EQ skills in your personal and marital life?

4. Discuss the role of emotional intelligence in stress management and resilience. How do individuals with high EQ cope with adversity and maintain psychological well-being?

5. Examine the influence of familial, cultural, and societal factors on the development and expression of emotional intelligence. How do familial and cultural norms and values shape emotional expression and regulation?

6. Share your cultural *"norms"* that may differ from those of your spouse and how that impacts your relationship with each other and your extended family.

Unconscious Bias

Unconscious bias is an area that only a few are aware of. Hence, the term *"unconscious bias."* So, what is unconscious bias, you ask? The word *"conscious"* describes a state of being aware of and responsive to one's surroundings. It involves being attuned to the environment and events around oneself. On the other hand, "unconscious" refers to the inability to be aware of one's surroundings and environment. Unconsciousness means not being aware of one's actions or their meanings and implications.

The Harvard Business Review defines and categorizes unconscious bias as follows: *"A snap judgment we make about people and situations based on years of subconscious socialization."* The human brain is hard-wired to make quick decisions that draw on a variety of assumptions and experiences without us even knowing it is doing so, meaning that our unconscious predispositions can influence our decision-making:

1) **Implicit biases** are not consciously created; rather, they stem from our brain's perception of what is normal, acceptable, or positive. These biases are shaped by various factors, including past experiences, cultural environment, and the influence of our social communities and media.
2) **Explicit bias** refers to attitudes and beliefs that we are fully aware of based on our perceptions. These biases are usually directed towards specific groups of people.
3) **Unconscious or Implicit Bias:** These biases are unintended, subtle, and subconscious associations that we learn through past experiences. They are thoughts that occur without our awareness on a conscious level.[20]

---

[20]Harvard School of Public Health. Office of Employee Development and Wellness. https://www.hsph.harvard.edu/wp-content/uploads/sites/2597/2022/06/

Bias refers to an attitude of prejudice towards others, whether they are people, events, ideas, or things that align with our existing frame of reference or presuppositions. Our experiences or lack thereof with such individuals, events, or concepts may prevent us from viewing them as unfamiliar or alien to our worldview. As a result, we may pre-judge them without fully understanding who or what they truly are.

Unconscious biases can significantly impact marriage relationships, often manifesting after the initial rush of romance and the honeymoon period. Many couples enter into marriage without fully understanding or being conscious of their partner's background, personality traits, family dynamics, and cultural differences. These unconscious biases, formed by past experiences, societal norms, and personal beliefs, can lead to misunderstandings, conflicts, and challenges in the relationship.

When couples fail to recognize or address these unconscious biases, they may find themselves caught up in patterns of blame, shame, finger-pointing, and accusations. This behavior can undermine trust, communication, and mutual respect, ultimately affecting the fulfillment of the vows they made to each other before God and witnesses.

Overcoming unconscious bias in marriage and in relationships in general begins with acknowledging and becoming aware of our biases. As the saying goes, *"What you do not know can hurt you."* One prevalent unconscious bias we all have is making assumptions. For instance, in intra-cultural marriages, there is an assumption that spouses should inherently understand each other's expectations due to their shared cultural background. In inter-cultural marriages, there can be an assumption that since they are willing to marry each other, they should already be knowledgeable about each other's cultures.

However, these assumptions often overlook the profound impact of cultural and familial upbringing on individuals' worldviews, attitudes, and behaviors. Pastors and pastoral counselors sometimes fail to recognize these differences and how they influence couples' interactions and expectations within the marriage.

This hidden yet significant issue affects all of us and can be a major factor in marital challenges. To reduce unnecessary conflicts, we must recognize and acknowledge our biases. We need to admit them, take ownership of them, and be open to others' feedback for our own growth and improvement.

How do we achieve this? It's beneficial to pause and apply the 4L principles mentioned earlier in this discussion:

1) **Lean In:** Take a proactive approach with your spouse by leaning into the relationship. Ensure they feel your presence and engagement.

2) **Listen To:** Actively listen to your spouse. Show them that you are attentive and genuinely interested. Listening involves understanding beyond just hearing responses, focusing on their reasons and emotions.

3) **Learn From:** Use the insights gained from listening to understand your spouse's perspectives and actions better. This understanding helps you learn about yourself and your reactions and enhances mutual understanding.

4) **Lead Forward:** By leaning in, listening attentively, and learning from your spouse, you pave the way for improved communication, nurturing the relationship, and deepening your connection over time.

Further Conversations

1. Define unconscious bias according to your own understanding and provide examples of how it can manifest in various contexts, such as crosscultural perception and interaction, interpersonal relationships, and decision-making processes.

2. Discuss strategies for identifying and mitigating unconscious biases in individuals, families, and cultures. Identify your *"blindspots"* both in thinking and doing in the context of your marriage relationship.

3. Without consciousness, can any strategies be formed to mitigate unconscious biases in our marriage and family relationship journey?

4. How can you improve your emotional intelligence so that you can engage with your spouse more effectively without unwanted confrontation in your communication?

Self-talk - Self-Reflection/Evaluation

Self-talk is an internal dialogue that everyone engages in, reflecting our need to communicate with ourselves. It's an essential process that requires our awareness. In their book *"The Sacred Romance,"* Brent Curtis and John Eldredge emphasize that from a very young age, life teaches us to ignore and distrust the deepest yearnings of our hearts. Society often encourages us to suppress our inner longings and instead prioritize external achievements like efficiency and performance.

Throughout our upbringing—from parents and peers to school, work, and spiritual mentors—we're subtly instructed to offer what is functional rather than authentic to our deepest selves. We're seldom encouraged to live from our hearts but rather to present carefully crafted personas aimed at gaining acceptance based on societal values. If we possess wealth, we're valued for our money; if beauty, for our appearance; if intelligence, for our intellect. This societal conditioning can lead us to divorce ourselves from our true essence, living a dual existence where we hide parts of ourselves to conform and gain approval.[21]

Taking time for self-reflection and self-talk is essential for personal growth and well-being. It provides an opportunity to connect with yourself, understand your thoughts and feelings, and clarify your goals and values. During self-reflection, strive to be open and honest. Recognize your strengths and areas for improvement without judgment. Reflect on what you're grateful for, the challenges you're encountering, and how you can navigate them. Be compassionate towards yourself and celebrate your achievements as you progress.

What is *"Self-talk?"* Self-talk is the way you talk to yourself or your inner voice. You might not be aware that you're doing it, but

---

[21]Curtis, Brent and Eldredge, John. The Sacred Romance: Drawing Closer to the Heart of God. Thomas Nelson Publishers, Nashville, TN. 1997, page 5.

you almost certainly are. This inner voice combines conscious thoughts with inbuilt beliefs and biases to create an internal monologue throughout the day.[22] Self-talk can have negative impacts on our lives because it leads to self-evaluation, which can lead to either self-elevation or self-degradation.

First, negative self-talk can be deeply impactful, influencing how we perceive ourselves based on various factors such as upbringing, background, personality, appearance, and cultural expectations. In contexts like the Hmong culture, for instance, some women may lament being born female due to societal norms that assign greater value to male roles within the family. This type of negative thinking and self-talk can contribute to feelings of self-devaluation and, ultimately, self-degradation. These internal dialogues, if unchecked, can hinder personal growth and maturity by undermining self-esteem and confidence. Recognizing and challenging negative self-talk is essential for fostering a healthier self-perception and promoting personal development.

Secondly, positive self-talk is crucial. Scripture reminds us in Romans 12:3,

"not to think more highly of ourselves than we ought, but to think of ourselves with sober judgment, according to the faith God has distributed to each of us."

Thinking soberly about ourselves means recognizing that Christ rescued and redeemed us. As the Lord is our Shepherd, we lack nothing, even amidst life's challenges. Our security and worth are rooted in our identity in Christ alone, not in seeking validation from others. Knowing that we are accepted as beloved children of God and co-heirs with Christ, we understand that our work for the Lord flows from our already established position in Him. It's crucial not to confuse our position in Christ with our performance.

---

[22]Self-talk is essential if we know how to do it. Examples of self-talk in Scripture are found in the Book of Psalms. One such example is Psalm 23 where David was talking to himself to reassure him that "The Lord is my Shepherd. I shall not be in want…"

Our position is secure through Christ, and our actions are a reflection of that position, not the other way around.

Os Guinness, in his book *"The Call,"* emphasizes the profound importance of personal identity with the following statement:

"For each of us, our own identity matters supremely. Whatever other people think, whatever current philosophies say, whatever the ups and downs of life may suggest, we intuitively act and think as if we have supreme value."

He further illustrates this concept by quoting Simone Weil, who writes, 'We possess nothing in this world other than the power to say, *"I."*[23] This self-identification is self-affirming, leading to a secure self-identity that believers find in Jesus Christ.

It is crucial that our self-talk remains balanced and rooted in our identity in Christ. Through Christ, we are transformed into new creations; the old has passed away, and the new has come (II Corinthians 5:17). Our identity is established through the merit of Jesus' sacrificial death, burial, and resurrection, as articulated by the apostle Paul:

"The life I now live in the body, I live by faith in the Son of God, who loved me and gave himself for me" (Galatians 2:20).

---

[23] Guinness, Os. The Call: Finding and Fulfilling the Central Purpose of Your Life. W Publishing Group, A Division of Thomas Nelson. Nashville, TN. 1998. P. 18.

Further Conversations

1. What are the key themes and principles of healing and wholeness presented in the book?

2. How does the author define healing and wholeness in marriage and family? Discuss the importance of this definition and how our understanding impacts our practice.

3. Explore the role of communication in fostering healing and wholeness within marriages and families. What strategies are suggested for improving communication dynamics?

4. How does the book address conflict resolution within marriages and families? Identify practical techniques or approaches recommended by the author. What would you do differently if you had to do it over again?

5. Discuss the significance of forgiveness and reconciliation in the context of marriage and family healing and wholeness. How are these concepts explored and applied in the book? How significant is the impact of forgiveness on the forgiver as opposed to the forgiven?

6. Analyze the influence of past experiences and family dynamics on present relationships. How does the book suggest addressing and overcoming past traumas or challenges?

7. Explore the intersection of spirituality and family healing and wholeness in the book. How does the author integrate spiritual principles into the healing process?

8. Reflect on the role of individual growth and self-awareness in fostering healthy relationships within marriages and families. What insights does the book offer in this regard?

9. Discuss the challenges and opportunities cultural and societal factors present in pursuing marriage and family healing. How does the book address cultural and family diversity and its impact on relationships?

10. Evaluate the practical exercises or activities provided in the book for promoting healing and wholeness in marriages and families. Which ones resonate most with you, and why?

Facilitating Cross-cultural and Cross-ethnic Marriages to Flourishing

Over the last fifty-plus years, cross-cultural, cross-ethnic, and even cross-religious marriages have become more common worldwide due to ongoing migrations. Interracial and inter-ethnic marriages were illegal in many countries until recently. In America, there were various reasons for these anti-miscegenation laws, including social and economic status differences or class distinctions.

"Anti-miscegenation laws," which banned white people from marrying Black and other non-white partners, have a long history in this country, often predating the creation of the U.S. Northern and Southern states alike passed these laws during the colonial era and throughout the nation's early decades. By the start of the Civil War in 1861, 28 states had enacted interracial marriage bans, and an additional seven states passed similar laws before the war ended in 1865.[24]

One of the main reasons for this rationale was that inter-racial and cross-ethnic marriages were deemed unnatural and, therefore, were incompatible between cultures and classes.[25] There were stigmas put on cross-cultural, cross-ethnic married couples and their families, including social, economic, and educational statuses.[26] The question that arises in our minds is, *"Why does society deem interracial and cross-cultural courtship and marriages unnatural?"* The unconscious prejudice of human

---

[24]www.eji.org/article, "To Prevent Interracial Marriage, California Requires That Marriage Licenses Indicate Race."

[25]Provost, Tylor. "History in the Making." California State University San Bernardino, Vol. 16, 2023.

[26]Dean, Tyler. "The Question of the Purpose of Anti-Miscegenation Laws." *Merge*, vol. 6, Iss. 1 2022. https://athenacommons.muw.edu/merge/vol6/iss1/1

sinful nature is demonstrated through our behaviors. The moment one of our family members is suspected of courting cross-culturally or cross-racially, our defensive antennas rise to their highest level because they have crossed the *"natural"* boundaries into unknown territories. This causes fear and anxiety, especially in the hearts and minds of parents and close family members. As a result of these fear factors, legal systems against interracial, cross-cultural, and cross-ethnic courtships and marriages came into existence.

According to a May 14, 2012, Huffington Post article titled *"Interracial Marriage Statistics: Pew Report Finds Mixed-Race Marriage Rates Rising,"* the 1980 Census, the first to collect data on interracial marriage, reported that 3% of all married couples were from different races. By 2010, this number had risen to 8.4%, which equates to one in twelve couples. When examining marriages recorded between 2008 and 2010, the statistics show that 22% of newly married couples in Western states were of different races or ethnicities, compared to 14% in the South, 13% in the Northeast, and 11% in the Midwest.[27]

As our nation continues to diversify each day and inter-racial, intercultural, and even inter-religious courtships become more common, it appears that the specific needs of cross-cultural and cross-ethnic marriages and families may not have received adequate attention from the majority of pastoral counselors. Therefore, addressing this subject constructively is crucial to assist couples and families in thriving and flourishing in these diverse contexts.

We have multicultural marriages within our family. My wife and I have daughters who are married to partners from different cultures—Hispanic American and Karen American. Additionally, extended family members have spouses who are non-Hmong, including African American and other European descent. Through

---

[27] https://www.sharetngov.tnsosfiles.com/tsla/exhibits/blackhistory/pdf.

these experiences, we have been challenged and enriched in our cross-cultural relationships, not only within our family circle but also within the broader community. These marriages have broadened our perspectives and deepened our understanding of diversity and cultural differences.

Cross-cultural and cross-ethnic marriages are not solely a modern phenomenon; they have roots in ancient times, even within the context of the Bible. From a Christian perspective, the Bible provides examples of such marriages. While the Bible generally discourages cross-religious marriages due to concerns about spiritual unity, there are exceptions.

For instance, Joseph, in Genesis 41:50-51, married Asenath, the daughter of an Egyptian priest from On. Similarly, Moses, as recorded in Exodus 2:21, married Zipporah, the daughter of a Midianite priest. These marriages were indeed cross-cultural and potentially cross-religious, yet both Joseph and Moses, through God's grace, were able to lead their wives toward acknowledging the God of Israel. As a result, their wives embraced the God of their husbands and supported them in fulfilling their divine callings.

These marriages had significant impacts on Joseph's and Moses' lives, their extended families, and their respective people. They illustrate how God can work through cross-cultural unions to bring about unity and mutual spiritual growth, ultimately leading to flourishing within families and communities.

In Solomon's time, his fame and wealth as the King of Israel allowed him to act freely as he grew older. From an Eastern perspective, Solomon's marriages to numerous foreign women likely had political motivations. Marrying these foreign women was a strategic move to maintain political peace with neighboring nations. Solomon aimed to reduce potential conflicts with these nations by becoming relatives through marriage.

Initially, Solomon's marriages may have been driven by political considerations, leveraging his wisdom granted by the Lord his God. However, as Solomon aged and accumulated more power, he exceeded the boundaries set by God. Following is what Scripture says about Solomon:

> *"King Solomon, however, loved many foreign women besides Pharaoh's daughter—*
>
> *Moabites, Ammonites, Edomites, Sidonians, and Hittites. They were from nations about which the Lord had told the Israelites, 'You must not intermarry with them because they will surely turn your hearts after their gods. Nevertheless, Solomon held fast to them in love. He had seven hundred wives of royal birth and three hundred concubines, and his wives led him astray. As Solomon grew old, his wives turned his heart to other gods, and his heart was not fully devoted to the Lord his God, as the heart of David, his father had been. He followed Ashtoreth, the goddess of the Sidonians, and Molek, the detestable God of the Ammonites. So Solomon did evil in the eyes of the Lord; he did not follow the Lord completely, as David his father had done"* –
> (I Kings 11:1-6) (Emphasis added).

Solomon violated God's first Commandment to *"love the Lord your God with all your heart, and with all your mind, and with all your soul, and with all your strength"* – (Deuteronomy 6:5). Instead, he "loved many foreign women besides Pharaoh's daughter..." Solomon's first wife was Egyptian, Pharoas' daughter. From this, we can assume that Solomon's first marriage was cross-cultural, and Scripture seems to be silent on it. His polygamy and cross-cultural and cross-religious marriages led him to compromise his relationship with his God and away from the God of his father David, who loved him and gave him what he had asked for - wisdom to rule the kingdom and wealth to make him have a comfortable lifestyle.

In the New Testament, Paul advises Christians not to form deep partnerships with unbelievers, even among those within the same cultural and ethnic groups. He states,

"Do not be yoked together with unbelievers. For what do righteousness and wickedness have in common? Or what fellowship can light have with darkness? What harmony is there between Christ and Belial? Or what does a believer have in common with an unbeliever? What agreement is there between the temple of God and idols?" (II Corinthians 6:14-16).

These rhetorical questions emphasize that there is no common ground between followers of Christ and those who worship idols or do not share the same faith. Therefore, Scripture is unequivocal regarding spiritual relationships, particularly in the context of marriage across religious boundaries. There is no room for compromise in spiritual relationships when it comes to marrying outside one's faith.

On the other hand, God used non-Jewish, non-Israelite women as instruments of salvation in several biblical stories: Judah and Tamar (Genesis 38), Salmon and Rahab (Matthew 1:5; Hebrews 11:31), Boaz and Ruth (Boaz being a child of a mixed marriage between Salmon and Rahab) (Ruth 1-4), and David and Bathsheba (2 Samuel 11). Through these narratives, the Word of God resoundingly declares,

"'Not by might nor by power, but by My Spirit,' says the Lord Almighty" (Zechariah 4:6).

Thus, not all cross-cultural and cross-ethnic marriages are negative or bad. By His grace and mercy, the Lord can use such marriages to advance the gospel in ways that monocultural marriages cannot. Scripture and history demonstrate the effectiveness of cross-cultural and cross-ethnic missionary couples in proclaiming the gospel throughout the world.

The point is genuine love should not be restricted or forbidden by anyone. Even in Scripture, God did not condemn genuine love solely based on religious differences. The primary concern God had about the Israelites marrying foreign women was the potential for religious apostasy. As Scripture states,

> *"Judah has been unfaithful. A detestable thing has been committed in Israel and in Jerusalem: Judah has desecrated the sanctuary the LORD loves by marrying women who worship a foreign god."* (Malachi 2:11) (emphasis added).

Therefore, there is nothing inherently wrong with cross-cultural, cross-racial, or cross-ethnic marriages as long as there is compatibility in religious affiliation and commitment.

In my premarital and marital counseling sessions with couples, I prioritize exploring their motivations for marriage and their reasons for seeking premarital counseling. This initial engagement allows me to assess their understanding of relationship compatibility and their readiness to compromise. I also guide them to reflect on how embracing Jesus Christ as Savior and Lord might impact their future together. This exploration helps couples consider the spiritual dimension of their relationship and the potential transformative effects of faith on their marital journey.

God is a jealous God who will not let the guilty go unpunished (Exodus 34:7; Numbers 14:18; Nahum 1:3). Why? Because He is the creator and sustainer of life. Our duty as His people is to obey and love Him, as King Solomon puts it so clearly (Ecclesiastes 12:13). Whenever anyone disobeys His commandments and strays from Him, trouble will inevitably follow.

To minimize misunderstandings in cross-cultural marriages and families and promote flourishing, it's crucial to address and adjust across five key layers of barriers: cultural, ethnic, family, personality, and educational. These layers require recognition, acceptance, and proactive adjustment to foster dynamic relationships and flourishing outcomes.

One of the most beautiful examples of cultural, ethnic, family, and personality adaptation in Scripture is found in the story of Ruth, as recorded in the book named after her. The story begins with Elimelek and Naomi migrating to Moab due to a famine in Israel. While in Moab, their sons married Moabite women, which were cross-cultural and cross-religious marriages. Tragically, Elimelek and his sons passed away, prompting Naomi to return to Israel. She urged her daughters-in-law to return to their own families.

As the story continues, Orpah decides to return to her own family, but Ruth refuses, saying to Naomi,

"Don't urge me to leave you or to turn back from you. Where you go I will go, and where you stay, I will stay. Your people will be my people and your God my God. Where you die, I will die, and there I will be buried. May the LORD deal with me, be it ever so severely, if even death separates you and me" (Ruth 1:16-17).

Ruth's commitment to Naomi after the loss of her husband was so strong that she refused to leave her mother-in-law's side. Ruth's commitment to Naomi spanned geography – *"where you go I will go"* – and encompassed social, cultural, and religious aspects – *"your people will be my people and your God my God."* For a marriage relationship to flourish in the long haul, there must be strong and deep levels of commitment and covenant in cross-cultural, cross-racial, and cross-ethnic marriages.

1) The Cultural Layer

Over the last few decades, cultural dynamics have continued to evolve, leading to an increase in courtship and marriages between different cultures. As this trend grows, the need for cross-cultural understanding and acceptance among in-laws of different cultures is becoming increasingly important. How do couples from different cultures navigate their cultural differences to avoid misunder-standings and minimize the potential for irreconcilable conflicts? One thing is clear: being aware of one's own cultural identity, values, and mannerisms is critically important. One of the key questions to ask ourselves is,

"What are my cultural identity and values, and how do I act or react in certain situations that I may not be conscious of?"
Another important question to ask is, *"What has been and is the cultural norm of the person I am courting or intending to marry?"*

Furthermore, can I trust someone to guide me in navigating cross-cultural understanding, particularly to understand my spouse or future spouse's culture and how they act or react in certain situations?

Culture encompasses more than just food, clothing, and language; it also includes mannerisms such as attitudes, behaviors, actions, relatedness, and how we greet each other.

For example, how does each spouse relate to their nucleus and extended families? In these relationship circles, how does each person address the other, including gender and generations?

Relationships between in-laws and extended family members can impact marital relationships and vice versa. Understanding how to relate between men and women, position, gender roles, and age, of different cultures involves knowing cultural norms for greetings addressings.

In the majority of American culture, hugging is a common way of greeting, irrespective of gender or generation. Conversely, in other cultures, greetings may vary depending on gender and/or generation, with practices such as bowing or maintaining personal space.

Another cultural difference lies in how individuals address their in-laws. In the majority of American culture, daughters-in-law and sons-in-law typically address their parents-in-law by their first names. However, in some cultures, it is customary for daughters-in-law and sons-in-law to address their parents-in-law as *"Mom"* and *"Dad,"* signifying a closer familial bond.

Although these differences may appear insignificant, they can lead to misunderstandings if not openly discussed and understood. Failing to address these cultural nuances can result in accusations of disrespect towards each other's parents or cultural norms.

Therefore, couples embarking on cross-cultural courtships and marriages must consider and discuss these aspects early on. By acknowledging and respecting each other's cultural practices, they can navigate potential misunderstandings and build a foundation of mutual understanding and respect within their relationship. These discussions are crucial for fostering harmony and longevity in their partnership.

2) The Ethnic Layer

As global political and religious unrest increases migration worldwide, more people are making America their home and establishing their lives across the nation. The necessity for cross-cultural, ethnic, and religious understanding is becoming increasingly evident. Young people from diverse ethnic and religious backgrounds often come together in classrooms and neighborhoods, fostering friendships across cultural lines. These casual friendships can evolve into courtships and, eventually, marriages and families over time. However, ethnic differences can become divisive issues within families if not addressed properly.

This responsibility falls on the shoulders of pastors and pastoral counselors. Are we equipped to engage with these issues effectively?

3) The Family Layer

In addition to considering cultural and ethnic backgrounds, we must also reflect on our family upbringing and how it shapes our adult lives. Personally, I've recognized the profound influence of my upbringing, particularly after my father passed away when I was just three years old. Raised by my mother as a single parent among six boys, I naturally adopted her mannerisms, speech patterns, behaviors, and even eating habits. Our family was notably boisterous, a trait inherited from my maternal grandparents, uncles, and aunts. As children, we didn't fully grasp the concept of *"like parents, like children"* until my pastoral counseling ministry shed light on how closely I mirrored my mother's behavior.

Unless and until we recognize how our attitudes and actions have been influenced by our family upbringing, we won't have the ability to consider changing our behaviors. This awareness is crucial because, without it, we might become defensive or offended when others point out aspects of our behavior that we don't like.

4) The Personality layer

Our personalities can significantly impact our relationships with our spouses. Some people are naturally more talkative than others, while others are more laid-back than their spouses. Differences in levels of extroversion or introversion can also play a role, where one spouse may be more outgoing while the other is quieter. While this isn't scientifically proven, my pastoral counseling experience over the years, including working with cross-ethnic and cross-cultural marriages, has shown that many challenges couples face stem from these various layers of identity and personality.

5) The Educational layer

Education is often seen as a pathway to better economic opportunities and improved lifestyles. The more educated a person is, the higher their earning potential and the better their standard of living compared to those with less education. However, education can sometimes hinder marital and familial flourishing. I have witnessed numerous marriages break down simply because one spouse is more educated than the other. The more educated partner, consciously or unconsciously, may unintentionally intimidate their spouse without considering their feelings. This dynamic cuts across both intra-cultural and inter-cultural marriages.

Individuals who exhibit this behavior often struggle with low self-esteem and may experience an identity crisis. They tie their self-worth and identity closely to their level of education and professional status, often overlooking the importance of their spouse's feelings and perspective. Ultimately, in the grand scheme of things, what matters most to a person should be their relationship with their spouse rather than external markers of success or status.

These questions are crucial for cross-cultural and cross-ethnic marriages to consider: Have you ever compared your level of education to your spouse's, whether consciously or unconsciously? If so, what went through your mind? When discussing finances, how often do you and your spouse talk about your respective incomes and compare them to the contributions each of you makes toward your daily living expenses?

The question is, how can we overcome such barriers so that cross-cultural and cross-ethnic marriages can flourish and thrive? One of the most important lessons I have learned is that as a minority living and serving within majority cultures, our cultural context doesn't define us exclusively. When engaging with people from backgrounds different than our own, we inevitably become the minority. Therefore, it's crucial to first be conscious of our own identity. This reminds me of Dorothy's words to Otto when they were *"swept away by the tornado and dropped into the Land of Oz"* — *"This is not Kansas anymore, Otto."* Similarly, in unfamiliar environments, we must be aware of our surroundings and learn to adapt effectively in order to function well.

The natural reaction in unfamiliar environments is often to keep our guard up. This attitude stems from feeling like a minority, where our opinions may not be valued, leading us to remain silent and withhold our thoughts. However, this approach doesn't positively contribute to our marriages. Instead, it can hinder and strain relationships with our cross-cultural partners and extended families.

My ministry experience in various cross-cultural contexts over the past three decades has taught me a valuable lesson: to advance God's kingdom effectively, I must bring my whole, redeemed self into my engagements. For a long time, I believed that as a minority in a majority culture, I should stay silent to avoid being seen as insignificant or being too aggressive or intrusive. Stay quiet is the way to stay engaged. As I get older, though, that's not true. As a member of my community, I must stay actively engaged because I can contribute to the improvement and advancement of my community. My counsel to cross-cultural and cross-ethnic married couples is be conscious of yourself and the space you are in. Be actively involved and interact within and outside of your own cultural/ethnic upbringing. Never stop learn, even your own culture.

As I continue to serve in multicultural settings, I've come to understand that stewarding God's gifts requires me to contribute actively to the flourishing of the Body of Christ. Holding back what I know and have been given would be akin to *"burying"* the talents entrusted to me.

Let me challenge cross-cultural and cross-ethnic couples to bring your fully redeemed selves into your relationships. Take the time to know each other as romantic partners and as beloved children of God. As you deepen your understanding of each other, you'll naturally enrich your interpersonal connection. This deeper connection will extend to your extended families on both sides, fostering a sense of belonging in both cultural contexts.

Embrace who you are without fear of embarrassment. Engage authentically, knowing that your unique perspectives and backgrounds contribute to the richness of your relationship.

Bringing your fully redeemed self to your marriage is crucial, not just for the relationship between you and your spouse, but for the flourishing of your extended families and future generations. Your marriage isn't isolated; it impacts your children, grandchildren, and beyond. Therefore, grounding your marriage in Biblical principles is essential for its longevity and positive influence on successive generations.

Marriage must be based on biblical love. We are reminded again of Paul's words to the Corinthians as recorded in 1 Corinthians 13:1-3:

> *"If I speak in the tongues of men or of angels, but do not have love, I am only a resounding gong or a clanging cymbal. If I have the gift of prophecy and can fathom all mysteries and all knowledge, and if I have a faith that can move mountains but do not have love, I am nothing. If I give all I possess to the poor and give over my body to hardship that I may boast, but do not have love, I gain nothing."* To sum up Paul's words: receiving gifts, acquiring knowledge, and giving generously—all must be connected to and extended by LOVE. Without love, everything we do is meaningless, *"a chasing after the wind."*

Further Conversations

1. **Cultural Layer:**

    - How does cultural background influence perceptions of marriage roles and responsibilities?

    - What are some common cultural practices regarding marriage ceremonies and rituals, and how do they impact marital dynamics?

    - How does culture influence attitudes towards divorce and marital conflict resolution?

    - In what ways does cultural identity affect partner selection and relationship expectations?

    - How do cultural norms regarding gender roles impact marital satisfaction and longevity?

    - How can cross-cultural spouses encourage each other to *"bring their fully redeemed selves"* into the culture to contribute the most to their marriage and family flourish?

2. **Ethnic Layer:**

    - What unique challenges do couples from different ethnic backgrounds face in their marriages?

- How do cultural values within ethnic communities shape marital expectations and behaviors?

- What role does extended family play in marriages within specific ethnic groups?

- How do traditions and customs from different ethnic backgrounds influence conflict resolution strategies in marriages?

- How do intercultural marriages navigate issues related to identity, language, and cultural integration?

3. **Family Layer**:

   - How does the family of origin influence individuals' perceptions of marriage and relationships?

   - What impact do family dynamics, such as communication patterns and conflict resolution styles, have on marital relationships?

   - How do family traditions and rituals shape married life and decision-making processes?

   - What role do extended family members play in marital conflicts and support systems?

- How does the quality of the relationship between spouses and their in-laws affect marital satisfaction?

4. **Personality Layer**:

    - How do personality traits, such as introversion/extroversion and agreeableness, influence marital dynamics?

    - What role does emotional intelligence play in maintaining a healthy marriage?

    - How do differences in personality between partners contribute to marital conflict or harmony?

    - How do attachment styles affect the way individuals form and maintain relationships within marriage?

    - How can understanding personality differences enhance communication and empathy within marriages?

5. **Educational Layer**:

    - How does educational attainment impact marital satisfaction and stability?

    - What role does financial stability, influenced by education, play in marital relationships?

- How do educational backgrounds influence parenting styles and decisions within marriages?

- How does access to education affect marital power dynamics and decision-making processes?

- What are the effects of disparities in educational levels between partners on marital communication and conflict resolution?

All scriptures are from the NIV, Digital version, www.BibleGateway.com and the NIV Hard Cover Version, The Holy Bible, New International Version, © Copyright 1973, 1978, 1984 by International Bible Society, and 1986, 1994 by the Moody Bible Institute of Chicago.

Biblegateway.com is a great resource for those who desire to have a consistent time in the Word of God without flipping through the pages of a hard copy of the Bible.

Afterwords

What does all of this mean? Words have meaning, and how we use them matters. More significantly, putting words into action is much more challenging; as the saying goes: *"Easier said than done."* As I have recently learned, truth passes through three stages. First, it is met with indifference. When the truth is first spoken, people often brush it off as nonsense, paying little attention to its meaning. Then, as they hear the truth again, their reaction changes dramatically over time. They shift from indifference to defensively reactive as the truth begins challenging and discomforting them.

As the truth continues to be presented over time, people's initial indifference often evolves into a defensive reaction. Eventually, in the third stage, they begin to let go. They realize that what was initially perceived as negative or offensive is not as bad as they thought. At this point, they learn to release their defensive attitudes. Embracing the truth means understanding its meaning and no longer seeing it as a threat but as something they can trust and support. I call these stages IDLES, which represent the journey we all take to arrive at acceptance. Reflecting on this, when was the last time you heard the truth for the first time and simply embraced it without question?

It's likely that only a few individuals readily and willingly accept the truth without any initial questions or opposition. In fact, people who accept things without conducting research or confirming facts are often labeled as naive and undiscerning. Society tends to apply these labels quickly.

For some individuals, accepting the truth comes more easily, while for others, the journey can be significantly challenging, and persisting in denial can have detrimental consequences. Moving from indifference to support is a journey that varies in length; some may traverse it in days or weeks, whereas for others, it may span a lifetime. It's important not to underestimate or trivialize the stages of this journey, which I refer to as our IDLES.

Again, I am reminded of Jesus' words: *"You shall know the truth, and the truth shall set you free"* (John 8:32). We all desire freedom, yet often find ourselves trapped in prisons of our own making. Embracing the truth is key to breaking free from these confines. When we acknowledge and accept the truth, we experience true freedom.

I hope that as you reflect more deeply on your relationship with God, yourself, and your spouse, you will come to know God more intimately, understand yourself better, and appreciate your spouse on a deeper level. As you grow in understanding God's purpose and plan for marriage, this knowledge will extend beyond yourself to influence those around you. With increased understanding, you will be equipped to guide, disciple, and mentor others in their relationships. Your own relationships will be enriched, leading to a healthier and more fulfilling life, not just aiming for *"happily ever after"* but thriving and flourishing as a faithful steward of God's blessings.

I do not claim to have all the answers. However, for those who assist in marriage and relationship guidance—pastors, counselors, and coaches—I hope the principles outlined in this work will offer ideas on how to disciple and guide couples and families who seek your help. To couples embarking on their marital journeys, my prayer is that you would take the insights shared here, remain open-minded, and honestly evaluate your principles. Through this process, you can articulate your beliefs clearly with each other, broadening your perspectives and deepening your mutual understanding. As we engage in this way, conflicts between spouses may become less frequent and more constructive, leading our relationships to flourish and thrive.

We all need to remember that no one is an expert in everything. All of us are pilgrims, journeying heavenward. As we embark on this journey, we have the opportunity to learn with and from one another, serving those we journey alongside. What I offer here is simply wisdom and skills gained from years of personal and professional experiences—as a husband, pastor, family and couple mediator, and steward—which I hope can provide insight into your pastoral stewardship as you shepherd God's flock.

I am reminded of Solomon's words in Proverbs 27:17,

> *"As iron sharpens iron, so one person sharpens another."*

If Solomon, known for his wisdom, saw the value in such reminders, how much more should I seek to be sharpened by my brothers and sisters? Just as I have been sharpened by others, I aspire to be an *"iron"* that helps sharpen others in their journey.

Notes for Personal Reflections

About the Author

Txhaj Cawv (T. Cher) and his wife, Mai Yia, are missionaries with Cru (formerly Campus Crusade for Christ) in the City Neighbors Immigrants, Internationals, and Refugees division. Over the past four decades, they have dedicated their lives to serving Hmong and cross-cultural ministry contexts in Michigan and Minnesota.

Txhaj Cawv has been actively involved in the Hmong community in the Twin Cities for over 20 years. He is the Founder and Executive Director of Family & Youth Advancement Services and serves as a Bible teacher for Suab Moob Ntseeg Yexus, a radio broadcast on KTIS AM 900.

In addition to his local community involvement, Txhaj Cawv has volunteered extensively in various Christian and non-Christian organizations in the Twin Cities area for more than three decades. He has served as a Founding Board member of Twin Cities Academy Charter School, participated in events like Promise Keepers and the Billy Graham Crusade, and been involved with organizations such as Harvest Evangelism Lighthouse of Prayer, Kingdom Oil Foundation, Minnesota Prayer Breakfast, St. Paul Prayer Breakfast, National Day of Prayer Minnesota Chapter,

Bethel University Board of Trustees, MissionShift Board of Directors, Overseas Tribal Services, Arrive Ministries Board of Directors, and Hope Dental Clinic in St. Paul.

Txhaj Cawv is also actively engaged in teaching roles. He serves as part of the instructor team for the Perspectives on World Christian Movement in the North Central US Region and as a Pastoral Counseling instructor for the Hmong District of the Christian and Missionary Alliance's HCI (Hmong Christian Institute), teaching students nationally and internationally. He has also served as a pulpit filler in congregations of varying sizes across the Twin Cities and mentors emerging leaders in leadership development, both locally and internationally.

Txhaj Cawv and Mai Yia reside in Maplewood, Minnesota, along with most of their five biological and five covenanted children, and they are blessed with 17 grandchildren.

Txhaj Cawv finds fulfillment in being a friend and coach, offering a listening ear to those facing challenging life journeys.

His overarching desire is to steward the calling and commission God has placed on his life for the advancement of Christ's kingdom, following the principle of *"being all things to all people so by all possible means save some"* (I Corinthians 9:22).

For information, leadership coaching, cross-cultural consultation, or pastoral counseling/guidance, please contact:

Txhaj Cawv Moua
2235 County Road D East
Maplewood, MN 55109
Phone: (651) 503-0239
Email: t.cher.moua@cru.org
www.LinkedIn.com/T. Cher Moua
www.Facebook/T. Cher Moua

Additional publication by Txhaj Cawv
Crossing the River: One Man's Journey From Darkness to Light.
Inspiring Voices, Bloomington, Indiana. 2013.
Available on www.amazon.com or www.InspiringVoices.Com

www.ingramcontent.com/pod-product-compliance
Lightning Source LLC
Chambersburg PA
CBHW070501100426
42743CB00010B/1721